How to Use Instagram for Business in 2024

The Entrepreneur's Definitive Guide for Commercializing Instagram Today

Michelle J. Galloway

DISCLAIMER

How to Use Instagram for Business in 2024: The Entrepreneur's Definitive Guide for Commercializing Instagram Today

First edition.

TABLE OF CONTENTS

INTRODUCTION

THE EVOLUTION OF INSTAGRAM AND ITS BUSINESS POTENTIAL

Instagram, the visual-centric social media platform, has come a long way since its inception in 2010. What started as a simple photo-sharing app has evolved into a global phenomenon, revolutionizing the way businesses connect with their audience. To understand Instagram's impact on modern business, it's essential to delve into its fascinating history and the pivotal moment when Facebook acquired the platform.

The Birth of Instagram

Kevin Systrom, a Stanford University graduate, and Mike Krieger, a Brazilian-born software engineer, founded Instagram in 2010. Initially, the app was called Burbn, a location-based app that allowed users to share photos, as well as make plans and meet up with friends. However, Systrom and Krieger soon realized that the photo-sharing feature was the most popular aspect of the app, leading them to pivot and focus solely on developing Instagram.

The name "Instagram" was derived from a combination of "instant" and "telegram," reflecting the app's ability to instantly share moments from users' lives. On October 6, 2010, Instagram launched on the App Store, and within a month, it gained 1 million users.

Rapid Growth and Early Success

Instagram's user base grew exponentially, with 10 million users joining the platform by September 2011. The app's popularity was attributed to its unique filters, which gave users' photos a distinct, retro aesthetic. In April 2012, Instagram launched on Android, further expanding its reach.

By April 2012, Instagram had amassed 30 million users, with 1 billion photos shared on the platform. The app's engagement was unparalleled, with users spending an average of 257 minutes per month on the app.

The Acquisition by Facebook

On April 9, 2012, Facebook announced its acquisition of Instagram for a staggering $1 billion. At the time, Instagram had only 13 employees, making it one of the most significant acquisitions in tech history.

Mark Zuckerberg, Facebook's CEO, recognized Instagram's potential and wanted to integrate its features into Facebook's ecosystem. Systrom and Krieger continued to lead Instagram, with Zuckerberg promising to maintain the app's autonomy.

Post-Acquisition and Expansion

Following the acquisition, Instagram continued to grow at an unprecedented rate. In 2013, Instagram introduced video sharing, allowing users to post 15-second clips. The same year, Instagram launched Instagram Direct, a feature enabling users to send private messages.

In 2014, Instagram surpassed 200 million users, with 65% of online adults aged 18-29 using the platform. The app's advertising potential became increasingly apparent, leading Facebook to integrate Instagram into its advertising platform.

In 2015, Instagram launched its advertising platform, allowing businesses to create sponsored posts and stories. The same year, Instagram surpassed 400 million users, with 75% of online adults aged 18-29 using the platform.

The Rise of Instagram Stories and Reels

In 2016, Instagram launched Instagram Stories, a feature allowing users to post ephemeral content that disappears after 24 hours. The feature was a massive success, with 100 million users adopting Instagram Stories within the first two months.

In 2020, Instagram launched Reels, a feature similar to TikTok, allowing users to create short videos. Reels quickly gained popularity, with 50% of Instagram users engaging with the feature within the first month.

Instagram's history is a testament to innovation and strategic growth. From its humble beginnings as a photo-sharing app to its current status as a global social media powerhouse, Instagram has revolutionized the way businesses connect with their audience. As we move forward in 2024, it's clear that Instagram will continue to play a vital role in shaping the future of commerce and entrepreneurship.

RISE OF INSTAGRAM'S POPULARITY AND USER BASE

Instagram's ascent to becoming a social media behemoth is a remarkable story of innovation, strategic decision-making, and a deep understanding of user behavior. From its humble beginnings as a photo-sharing app to its current status as a global phenomenon, Instagram's popularity and user base have grown exponentially, making it an indispensable platform for businesses and entrepreneurs.

Early Adoption and Network Effects

Instagram's initial success can be attributed to its early adoption by influencers, photographers, and creatives. The app's unique filters and user-friendly interface made it an instant hit among this demographic. As more users joined the platform, the network effects took hold, and Instagram's popularity snowballed.

The app's viral growth was further fueled by its integration with Facebook, Twitter, and other social media platforms. Users could share their Instagram posts across multiple platforms, increasing the app's visibility and attracting new users.

Visual Storytelling and User Engagement

Instagram's focus on visual storytelling resonated with users, who were increasingly consuming and sharing content on their mobile devices. The app's emphasis on aesthetics, combined with its user-friendly editing features, made it easy for users to create engaging content that told stories about their lives, interests, and passions.

As users engaged with each other's content, Instagram's algorithm evolved to prioritize posts that generated high engagement, creating a virtuous cycle of user-generated content, engagement, and growth.

Influencer Marketing and Celebrity Endorsements

Instagram's popularity among influencers and celebrities played a significant role in its rapid growth. Influencers, who had built large followings on the platform, partnered with brands to promote products and services, further increasing Instagram's appeal to businesses and entrepreneurs.

Celebrity endorsements, such as Kim Kardashian's early adoption of the platform, also contributed to Instagram's mainstream appeal. As more celebrities joined the platform, Instagram became a go-to destination for fans and followers.

Expansion into New Features and Demographics

Instagram's expansion into new features, such as video sharing, Instagram Stories, and Reels, attracted new users and increased engagement among existing ones. The platform's foray into e-commerce, with the introduction of shopping tags and Instagram Checkout, further solidified its position as a commerce-driven platform.

Instagram's growth also extended to new demographics, as the platform became increasingly popular among older adults, businesses, and entrepreneurs. The app's user base expanded beyond its initial core of young adults, making it a more diverse and inclusive platform.

Global Expansion and Localization

Instagram's global expansion was strategic and deliberate, with the platform launching in new markets and languages. The app's localization efforts, such as the introduction of region-specific filters and features, helped to increase adoption in diverse markets.

Today, Instagram is available in over 30 languages, with a significant presence in markets such as the United States, Brazil, India, and Europe. The platform's global reach and localization efforts have made it an essential tool for businesses and entrepreneurs operating in diverse markets.

Instagram's rise to popularity and its massive user base are a testament to the platform's innovative approach to social media, its strategic decision-making, and its deep understanding of user behavior. As businesses and entrepreneurs continue to leverage Instagram's features and advertising platform, the app's growth and popularity are likely to continue, making it an indispensable tool for commercial success in 2024 and beyond.

INTRODUCTION OF BUSINESS FEATURES AND ADVERTISING OPTIONS

The introduction of business features and advertising options on Instagram marked a significant turning point in the platform's history. Prior to 2013, Instagram was primarily used as a social media platform for personal use. However, as the platform's popularity grew, Instagram began to shift its focus to also cater to businesses and entrepreneurs.

One of the first business features introduced by Instagram was the ability for users to switch to a business profile. This new profile type allowed businesses to access valuable insights about their followers and their posts' performance. With a business profile, businesses could see how many people were viewing their posts, how many likes and comments they were receiving, and even how many website clicks they were getting. This information was invaluable for businesses looking to understand their audience and tailor their content to meet their needs.

In addition to business profiles, Instagram also introduced Instagram Ads. Launched in 2015, Instagram Ads allowed businesses to create sponsored posts and stories that could reach a larger audience. These ads could be targeted based on demographics, interests, and behaviors, making them a powerful tool for businesses looking to increase brand awareness and drive website traffic. With Instagram Ads, businesses could reach people who were likely to be interested in their products or services, even if they weren't already following their account.

Another key feature introduced by Instagram was Instagram Stories. Launched in 2016, Instagram Stories allowed users to post ephemeral content that disappears after 24 hours. This feature quickly became popular among businesses, as it provided a new way to connect with customers and share behind-the-scenes content. With Instagram Stories, businesses could share sneak peeks of new products, give tours of their offices, or even share exclusive deals and discounts.

As Instagram's business features continued to evolve, the platform introduced Shopping Tags. Shopping Tags allowed businesses to tag products directly in their posts and stories, making it easy for customers to purchase products from businesses directly from the app. With Shopping Tags, businesses could tag products in their posts and stories, and customers could purchase those products by tapping on the tag.

In 2020, Instagram launched Reels, a feature similar to TikTok. Reels allowed users to create short videos that could be shared with their followers. Reels quickly became popular among businesses, as they provided a new way to create engaging content that could be shared with customers. With Reels, businesses could create short videos showcasing their products or services, share tutorials or tips, or even share customer testimonials.

Today, Instagram offers a wide range of business features and advertising options, including:

- Instagram Ads: allows businesses to create sponsored posts and stories that can reach a larger audience.

- Instagram Insights: provides businesses with insights about their followers and their posts' performance.
- Shopping Tags: allows businesses to tag products directly in their posts and stories.
- Reels: allows businesses to create short videos that can be shared with customers.
- Instagram Stories: allows businesses to post ephemeral content that disappears after 24 hours.
- Branded Content Ads: allows businesses to partner with creators to reach a larger audience.
- Instagram Live: allows businesses to connect with customers in real-time.
- IGTV: allows businesses to create long-form video content.
- Instagram Carousel: allows businesses to post multiple images and videos in a single post.
- Instagram's Shopping Cart: allows customers to purchase products directly from the app.

These features and advertising options have made Instagram an essential platform for businesses and entrepreneurs looking to commercialize their brand and reach a larger audience. With Instagram's business features, businesses can increase brand awareness, drive website traffic, and even sell products directly from the app.

Now that we've talked about these, let us go into discussing the process of setting up a business account on Instagram.

SETTING UP YOUR INSTAGRAM BUSINESS ACCOUNT

Creating a business profile on Instagram is a crucial step in establishing a professional presence on the platform. As an entrepreneur, having a business profile allows you to access valuable insights about your followers, promote your products or services, and connect with your customers in a more professional manner. In this section, we will provide a complete step-by-step guide on creating a business profile and converting from a personal account.

Step 1: Log in to Your Instagram Account

To create a business profile, you need to log in to your Instagram account. If you don't have an account, download the Instagram app and sign up for a new account.

Step 2: Tap the Profile Icon
Once you're logged in, tap the profile icon on the bottom right corner of the screen. This will take you to your profile page.

Step 3: Tap the Three Horizontal Lines
On your profile page, tap the three horizontal lines on the top right corner of the screen. This will open your account settings.

Step 4: Tap "Settings"
In your account settings, tap "Settings" to access your account options.

Step 5: Tap "Account"
In your account options, tap "Account" to access your account type.

Step 6: Tap "Switch to Business Profile"
In your account type, tap "Switch to Business Profile" to convert your personal account to a business profile.

Step 7: Connect Your Facebook Page
To create a business profile on Instagram, you need to connect your Facebook page. Tap "Connect Facebook Page" and select the page you want to connect.

Step 8: Choose Your Business Category
Once you've connected your Facebook page, choose your business category from the list of options.

Step 9: Add Your Business Information
Add your business information, including your business name, email address, phone number, and address.

Step 10: Review and Confirm
Review your business information and confirm that everything is accurate.

Step 11: Set Up Your Business Profile
Once you've confirmed your business information, set up your business profile by adding a profile picture, bio, and contact information.

Step 12: Access Your Business Insights
After setting up your business profile, access your business insights to see how your content is performing and engage with your followers.

VERIFYING YOUR ACCOUNT AND ADDING CONTACT INFORMATION

Verifying your account and adding contact information are crucial steps in establishing a professional presence on Instagram. As an entrepreneur, verifying your account and adding contact information helps to build trust with your audience, increases your credibility, and provides a way for customers to get in touch with you. In this section, we will provide a detailed guide on how to verify your account and add contact information on Instagram.

VERIFYING YOUR ACCOUNT

Verifying your account on Instagram is a simple process that helps to confirm your identity and build trust with your audience. To verify your account, follow these steps:

Step 1: Log in to Your Instagram Account
Log in to your Instagram account using your username and password.

Step 2: Tap the Profile Icon
Tap the profile icon on the bottom right corner of the screen to access your profile page.

Step 3: Tap the Three Horizontal Lines
Tap the three horizontal lines on the top right corner of the screen to access your account settings.

Step 4: Tap "Settings"
Tap "Settings" to access your account options.

Step 5: Tap "Account"
Tap "Account" to access your account type.

Step 6: Tap "Request Verification"
Tap "Request Verification" to submit a request for verification.

Step 7: Enter Your Information

Enter your name, email address, and a government-issued ID to confirm your identity.

Step 8: Submit Your Request
Submit your request for verification and wait for Instagram to review your application.

Step 9: Receive Your Verification
Once your application is approved, you will receive a notification from Instagram indicating that your account has been verified.

ADDING CONTACT INFORMATION

Adding contact information to your Instagram profile is an essential step in providing a way for customers to get in touch with you. To add contact information, follow these steps:

Step 1: Log in to Your Instagram Account
Log in to your Instagram account using your username and password.

Step 2: Tap the Profile Icon
Tap the profile icon on the bottom right corner of the screen to access your profile page.

Step 3: Tap "Edit Profile"
Tap "Edit Profile" to access your profile settings.

Step 4: Tap "Contact Information"
Tap "Contact Information" to add your contact details.

Step 5: Enter Your Contact Information
Enter your email address, phone number, and physical address to add your contact information.

Step 6: Save Your Changes
Save your changes to update your profile with your contact information.

Tips and Best Practices:

- Use a professional email address and phone number to represent your business.
- Add a physical address to provide a location for your business.
- Use a consistent format for your contact information across all social media platforms.
- Make sure your contact information is up-to-date and accurate.
- Use Instagram's built-in features, such as Instagram Direct, to communicate with customers and respond to inquiries.

By verifying your account and adding contact information, you can establish a professional presence on Instagram and provide a way for customers to get in touch with you. Remember to always keep your contact information up-to-date and accurate to ensure that customers can reach you easily.

PART 1

Instagram Basics

CHAPTER 1

NAVIGATION AND INTERFACE

UNDERSTANDING THE INSTAGRAM APP LAYOUT AND NAVIGATION

Instagram's app layout and navigation are designed to provide a seamless user experience, allowing you to easily create and share content, engage with your audience, and grow your business. As an entrepreneur, understanding the Instagram app layout and navigation is crucial to maximizing your presence on the platform. In this section, we'll delve into the details of the Instagram app layout and navigation, providing you with a comprehensive guide to help you navigate the platform like a pro.

Home Screen

The Home screen is the first thing you see when you open the Instagram app. It's a feed of posts from accounts you follow, including photos, videos, Stories, and Reels. The Home screen is personalized to show content that Instagram thinks you'll be interested in, based on your interactions and engagement history.

Navigation Bar

The Navigation bar is located at the bottom of the screen and provides access to the main features of the app. The Navigation bar consists of five icons:

- Home: Takes you to the Home screen
- Explore: Takes you to the Explore page, where you can discover new content and accounts
- Camera: Opens the camera, allowing you to take photos or videos

- Activity: Shows your account activity, including likes, comments, and mentions
- Profile: Takes you to your profile page

Profile Page

Your Profile page is where your audience can learn more about you and your business. It displays your profile picture, bio, and posts. You can also access your account settings and privacy options from this page.

Post Options

When you open a post, you'll see several options:

- Like: Tap the heart icon to like the post
- Comment: Tap the comment icon to leave a comment
- Share: Tap the share icon to share the post with others
- Save: Tap the save icon to save the post to your collection

Stories and Reels

Stories and Reels are features that allow you to create and share content that disappears after 24 hours. Stories appear at the top of the Home screen, and Reels appear in a separate tab on the Navigation bar.

Direct Messages

Direct Messages (DMs) allow you to privately communicate with other users. You can access DMs from the Navigation bar or from the Profile page.

Settings

The Settings page allows you to customize your account, including:

- Account settings: Edit your profile, change your password, and manage your account
- Privacy settings: Control who can see your content, who can contact you, and more
- Notifications: Customize your notification preferences

EXPLORING THE HOME FEED, EXPLORE PAGE, AND PROFILE PAGE

Instagram's home feed, Explore page, and profile page are essential components of the platform, providing users with a personalized experience tailored to their interests and interactions. As an entrepreneur, understanding how to navigate and utilize these features is crucial to maximizing your presence on Instagram and growing your business.

In this section, we'll delve into the details of the home feed, Explore page, and profile page, providing you with a comprehensive guide to help you commercialize Instagram today.

Home Feed

The home feed is the first thing you see when you open the Instagram app. It's a personalized feed of posts from accounts you follow, including photos, videos, Stories, and Reels. The home feed is designed to show content that Instagram thinks you'll be interested in, based on your interactions and engagement history.
The home feed is divided into several sections:

- Posts from accounts you interact with the most

- Posts from accounts you've recently interacted with
- Posts that are likely to engage you
- Sponsored posts from businesses

You can interact with posts in the home feed by liking, commenting, or sharing them. You can also use the "Not Interested" button to hide posts from accounts you don't want to see.

Explore Page

The Explore page is a discovery feature that shows you content from accounts you don't follow. It's designed to help you discover new accounts, hashtags, and interests. The Explore page is personalized based on your interactions and engagement history.

The Explore page is divided into several sections:

- Photos and videos from accounts you might be interested in
- Reels and Stories from accounts you might be interested in
- Hashtags and challenges related to your interests
- Sponsored posts from businesses

You can interact with content on the Explore page by liking, commenting, or sharing it. You can also use the "Not Interested" button to hide content that doesn't interest you.

Profile Page

Your profile page is your personal space on Instagram, where you can share information about yourself, your business, and your interests. Your profile page includes:

- Your profile picture and bio

- Your posts, including photos, videos, Stories, and Reels
- Your followers and following list
- Your account settings and privacy options

You can customize your profile page by adding a profile picture, bio, and contact information. You can also use Instagram's built-in features, such as Instagram Stories and Reels, to share behind-the-scenes content and sneak peeks.

CUSTOMIZING YOUR ACCOUNT SETTINGS AND NOTIFICATIONS

Customizing your account settings and notifications on Instagram is crucial to maximizing your presence on the platform and growing your business. As an entrepreneur, understanding how to tailor your account settings and notifications to your needs can help you stay focused, productive, and engaged with your audience. In this section, we'll delve into the details of customizing your account settings and notifications, providing you with a comprehensive guide to help you commercialize Instagram today.

ACCOUNT SETTINGS

Your account settings allow you to customize your profile, privacy, and security on Instagram. To access your account settings, follow these steps:

- Go to your profile page
- Tap the three horizontal lines on the top right corner
- Tap "Settings"
- Tap "Account"

From here, you can customize your:

- Profile information, including your name, email address, and password
- Privacy settings, including who can see your content, who can contact you, and more
- Security settings, including two-factor authentication and login activity
- Account type, including switching to a business or creator account

NOTIFICATIONS

Notifications allow you to stay up-to-date with activity on your account, including likes, comments, mentions, and more. To customize your notifications, follow these steps:

- Go to your profile page
- Tap the three horizontal lines on the top right corner
- Tap "Settings"
- Tap "Notifications"

From here, you can customize your notifications for:

- Posts, including likes, comments, and mentions
- Stories, including replies and mentions
- Reels, including likes, comments, and mentions
- Direct Messages, including messages and mentions
- Followers, including new followers and unfollowers

CHAPTER 2

CONTENT TYPES (POSTS, STORIES, REELS, IGTV, LIVE)

UNDERSTANDING THE DIFFERENT CONTENT FORMATS AND THEIR USES

Instagram offers a variety of content formats that allow businesses to showcase their products, services, and brand story in unique and engaging ways. As an entrepreneur, understanding the different content formats and their uses is crucial to creating a successful Instagram marketing strategy. In this section, we'll delve into the details of each content format, providing you with a comprehensive guide to help you commercialize Instagram today.

1. Feed Posts

Feed posts are the traditional posts that appear in your followers' feeds. They can be photos, videos, or carousels, and are ideal for sharing updates, promotions, and product showcases.

2. Instagram Stories

Instagram Stories are ephemeral content that disappears after 24 hours. They can be photos, videos, or boomerangs, and are ideal for sharing behind-the-scenes content, sneak peeks, and exclusive deals.

3. Reels

Reels are short videos that can be up to 60 seconds long. They can be used to create engaging content, showcase products, and provide tutorials.

4. IGTV

IGTV (Instagram TV) is a feature that allows users to upload longer-form videos up to 60 minutes. It's ideal for sharing in-depth content, product demos, and brand stories.

5. Instagram Live

Instagram Live allows users to broadcast live video content to their followers. It's ideal for hosting Q&A sessions, product launches, and exclusive events.

6. Carousels

Carousels are a type of feed post that allows users to upload multiple photos or videos in a single post. They're ideal for showcasing product collections, telling brand stories, and sharing customer testimonials.

7. Instagram Guides

Instagram Guides are a feature that allows users to curate content from their feed posts and stories into a single post. They're ideal for sharing product roundups, brand stories, and customer testimonials.

CREATING AND EDITING POSTS, STORIES, REELS, IGTV, AND LIVE STREAMS

Creating and editing content on Instagram is a crucial step in commercializing your brand and engaging with your audience. As an entrepreneur, understanding how to create and edit posts, stories, reels, IGTV, and live streams is essential to showcasing your products, services, and brand story in a unique and engaging way. In this section, we'll delve into the details of creating and editing content on Instagram, providing you with a comprehensive guide to help you commercialize Instagram today.

Posts

Creating a post on Instagram is a straightforward process. To create a post, follow these steps:

- Tap the "+" icon on the top right corner of your screen
- Select the photo or video you want to upload from your camera roll or take a new one
- Add a caption and hashtags
- Tag relevant accounts and locations
- Share your post

Editing a post is also easy. To edit a post, follow these steps:

- Tap the three horizontal lines on the top right corner of your post
- Tap "Edit"
- Make your changes, such as adding or removing hashtags, tagging accounts, or changing the caption
- Tap "Done" to save your changes

Stories

Creating a story on Instagram is similar to creating a post. To create a story, follow these steps:

- Tap the camera icon on the top left corner of your screen
- Select the photo or video you want to upload from your camera roll or take a new one
- Add text, drawings, or other effects
- Share your story

Editing a story is also easy. To edit a story, follow these steps:

- Tap the three horizontal lines on the top right corner of your story
- Tap "Edit"
- Make your changes, such as adding or removing text or effects
- Tap "Done" to save your changes

Reels

Creating a reel on Instagram is similar to creating a post. To create a reel, follow these steps:

- Tap the "+" icon on the top right corner of your screen
- Select the video you want to upload from your camera roll or record a new one
- Add audio and effects
- Share your reel

Editing a reel is also easy. To edit a reel, follow these steps:

- Tap the three horizontal lines on the top right corner of your reel
- Tap "Edit"
- Make your changes, such as adding or removing audio or effects
- Tap "Done" to save your changes

IGTV

Creating an IGTV video on Instagram is similar to creating a post. To create an IGTV video, follow these steps:

- Tap the "+" icon on the top right corner of your screen
- Select the video you want to upload from your camera roll or record a new one
- Add a title and description
- Share your IGTV video

Editing an IGTV video is also easy. To edit an IGTV video, follow these steps:

- Tap the three horizontal lines on the top right corner of your IGTV video
- Tap "Edit"
- Make your changes, such as adding or removing titles or descriptions
- Tap "Done" to save your changes

Live Streams

Creating a live stream on Instagram is similar to creating a post. To create a live stream, follow these steps:

- Tap the camera icon on the top left corner of your screen
- Select "Live" from the options
- Add a title and description
- Start your live stream

Editing a live stream is not possible, as it is a real-time video. However, you can save your live stream to your camera roll or IGTV after it ends.

CHAPTER 3

HASHTAGS AND TAGGING

UNDERSTANDING HOW HASHTAGS WORK AND THEIR IMPORTANCE

Hashtags are a crucial element on Instagram, allowing users to discover and engage with content related to specific topics or interests. As an entrepreneur, understanding how hashtags work and their importance is vital to commercializing your brand and reaching your target audience.

Instagram's hashtag system is a powerful tool for businesses, allowing them to increase visibility, engagement, and brand awareness. However, with millions of hashtags to choose from, it can be overwhelming to determine which ones to use and how to use them effectively. In this section, we'll delve into the details of hashtags, providing you with a comprehensive guide on how to harness their power to commercialize your Instagram presence.

What are Hashtags?

Hashtags are keywords or phrases preceded by the "#" symbol, used to categorize and make posts discoverable on Instagram. When a user searches for a hashtag, they'll see a feed of posts that have used that hashtag, allowing them to discover new content and accounts. Hashtags can be used in both posts and stories, and can be combined with other hashtags to reach a wider audience.

The History of Hashtags

Hashtags originated on Twitter in 2007, created by Chris Messina, a developer and Twitter user. Messina proposed using the "#" symbol to group related tweets together, making it easier for users to discover and engage with content. Since then, hashtags have become an integral part of social media platforms, including Instagram.

How Hashtags Work on Instagram

On Instagram, hashtags are used to categorize posts and make them discoverable by other users. When a user searches for a hashtag, they'll see a feed of posts that have used that hashtag, allowing them to discover new content and accounts. Instagram's algorithm uses hashtags to understand the content of a post and show it to users who are likely to engage with it.

How Do Hashtags Work?

When you use a hashtag in your post, it becomes searchable by other users who are interested in that topic. Instagram's algorithm uses hashtags to understand the content of your post and show it to users who are likely to engage with it. The algorithm takes into account the popularity of the hashtag, the engagement on your post, and other factors to determine its visibility.

For example, if you're a fashion brand and you use the hashtag #fashion, your post will be visible to users who have searched for that hashtag or have shown an interest in fashion-related content. The algorithm will also consider the engagement on your post, such as likes and comments, to determine how visible your post should be to other users.

Types of Hashtags

There are several types of hashtags, each with its own purpose and benefits:

- Niche hashtags: Specific to a particular industry or niche, these hashtags attract targeted audiences.
- Broad hashtags: General and widely used, these hashtags attract larger audiences.
- Branded hashtags: Unique to a particular brand, these hashtags build brand awareness and encourage user-generated content.
- Event hashtags: Used for events, conferences, and meetups, these hashtags connect attendees and create a community.

Importance of Hashtags

Hashtags are essential for businesses on Instagram, as they:

- Increase discoverability: Hashtags make your content visible to users who are searching for topics related to your business. This can help you reach a wider audience and attract new followers.
- Boost engagement: Using relevant hashtags can increase likes, comments, and shares on your posts. This can help you build a community around your brand and increase engagement with your content.
- Build brand awareness: Consistently using specific hashtags can help establish your brand's identity and reputation. This can help you build trust with your audience and increase brand loyalty.
- Attract new followers: Using popular and relevant hashtags can attract new followers who are interested in your content. This can help you grow your audience and increase your reach.

Tips for Using Hashtags

- Use relevant and specific hashtags: Use hashtags that are directly related to your content and target audience. This can help you attract users who are interested in your content and increase engagement.

- Use a mix of popular and niche hashtags: Using a combination of popular and niche hashtags can increase visibility and engagement. Popular hashtags can help you reach a wider audience, while niche hashtags can help you attract users who are specifically interested in your content.
- Use no more than 10 hashtags: Using too many hashtags can look spammy and may not be as effective. Stick to a few relevant hashtags that accurately describe your content.
- Create a branded hashtag: Create a unique hashtag for your business to build brand awareness and encourage user-generated content. This can help you build a community around your brand and increase engagement.

Best Practices for Hashtags

- Research popular hashtags in your niche: Use tools like Instagram's built-in search bar or third-party apps to research popular hashtags in your niche. This can help you find relevant hashtags that will attract users who are interested in your content.
- Use hashtags consistently across posts: Use the same hashtags consistently across your posts to build brand awareness and increase visibility. This can help you establish your brand's identity and reputation.
- Monitor hashtag performance using analytics tools: Use analytics tools like Instagram Insights to monitor the performance of your hashtags. This can help you determine which hashtags are most effective and adjust your strategy accordingly.
- Adjust hashtag strategy based on performance: Based on the performance of your hashtags, adjust your strategy to use more effective hashtags. This can help you increase engagement and attract new followers.

- Use hashtags in Instagram Stories and Reels: Use hashtags in your Instagram Stories and Reels to increase visibility and engagement. This can help you attract users who are interested in your content and increase brand awareness.

By understanding how hashtags work and their importance, you'll be able to harness their power to increase visibility, engagement, and brand awareness on Instagram. Remember to research relevant hashtags, use a mix of hashtags, limit hashtag use, and create a branded hashtag to establish your brand's presence on Instagram.

RESEARCHING AND USING RELEVANT HASHTAGS FOR YOUR BUSINESS

Hashtags are a crucial element in Instagram marketing, allowing businesses to increase visibility, engagement, and brand awareness. However, with millions of hashtags to choose from, it can be overwhelming to determine which ones to use and how to use them effectively. In this section, we'll delve into the details of researching and using relevant hashtags for your business, providing you with a comprehensive guide to help you commercialize your Instagram presence.

Researching Relevant Hashtags
Researching relevant hashtags is the first step in harnessing their power. Here are some tips to help you get started:

- Use Instagram's built-in search bar: Type in keywords related to your business to see suggested hashtags and their popularity.
- Utilize third-party apps: Tools like Hootsuite, Sprout Social, and Hashtagify provide comprehensive hashtag research and analytics.

- Analyze competitors: Research your competitors' hashtags and identify gaps in the market.
- Identify niche hashtags: Find specific hashtags related to your industry or niche.

Evaluating Hashtag Relevance

Not all hashtags are created equal. When evaluating hashtag relevance, consider the following factors:

- Popularity: Choose hashtags with a moderate level of popularity (1,000 to 100,000 uses).
- Relevance: Select hashtags directly related to your business or industry.
- Competition: Avoid overly competitive hashtags with millions of uses.
- Engagement: Opt for hashtags with high engagement rates (likes, comments, saves).

Using Relevant Hashtags

Once you've researched and evaluated relevant hashtags, it's time to use them effectively:

- Use a mix of broad and niche hashtags: Combine general and specific hashtags to attract a targeted audience.
- Limit hashtag use: Use no more than 10 hashtags per post to avoid looking spammy.
- Create a branded hashtag: Establish a unique hashtag for your business to build brand awareness and encourage user-generated content.
- Use hashtags consistently: Apply a consistent hashtag strategy across posts to establish your brand's identity.

Best Practices for Hashtag Research and Use

- Monitor hashtag performance: Use analytics tools to track hashtag performance and adjust your strategy accordingly.
- Avoid overused hashtags: Steer clear of overly popular hashtags that may not attract targeted audiences.
- Leverage user-generated content: Encourage followers to use your branded hashtag and re-share their content.
- Stay up-to-date with trends: Continuously research and update your hashtag strategy to stay relevant.

By researching and using relevant hashtags, you'll be able to increase visibility, engagement, and brand awareness on Instagram. Remember to evaluate hashtag relevance, use a mix of hashtags, limit hashtag use, and create a branded hashtag to establish your business's presence on Instagram.

TAGGING OTHER ACCOUNTS AND LOCATIONS IN YOUR CONTENT

Tagging other accounts and locations in your content is a powerful way to increase engagement, build relationships, and expand your reach on Instagram. As an entrepreneur, understanding how to tag effectively is crucial to commercializing your brand and growing your business. In this section, we'll delve into the details of tagging other accounts and locations, providing you with a comprehensive guide to help you commercialize your Instagram presence.

Tagging Other Accounts

Tagging other accounts in your content allows you to:

- Collaborate with influencers and partners
- Give shoutouts to loyal customers and supporters

- Engage with other businesses and brands
- Build relationships and networks

To tag another account, simply type the "@" symbol followed by the account's username. Instagram will suggest accounts as you type, making it easy to find and tag the right ones.

Tagging Locations

Tagging locations in your content allows you to:

- Geotag your business or event location
- Reach a local audience and attract foot traffic
- Share your travel and adventure experiences
- Connect with other users who have visited the same location

To tag a location, simply type the "@" symbol followed by the location's name. Instagram will suggest locations as you type, making it easy to find and tag the right ones.
Best Practices for Tagging

- Tag relevant accounts and locations: Only tag accounts and locations that are relevant to your content and audience.
- Use a mix of niche and broad tags: Combine specific and general tags to attract a targeted audience.
- Limit tag use: Use no more than 10 tags per post to avoid looking spammy.
- Tag consistently: Apply a consistent tagging strategy across posts to establish your brand's identity.

Benefits of Tagging

- Increased engagement: Tagging other accounts and locations can increase likes, comments, and shares on your posts.

- Expanded reach: Tagging can help your content reach a wider audience, including followers of the tagged accounts and locations.
- Building relationships: Tagging can help you build relationships with other businesses, influencers, and customers.
- Improved brand awareness: Consistent tagging can establish your brand's identity and reputation.

Tips for Effective Tagging

- Research relevant accounts and locations: Use Instagram's search bar and third-party apps to find relevant tags.
- Use a mix of tags: Combine account and location tags to attract a targeted audience.
- Monitor tag performance: Use analytics tools to track tag performance and adjust your strategy accordingly.
- Be authentic and genuine: Only tag accounts and locations that align with your brand's values and messaging.

By tagging other accounts and locations in your content, you'll be able to increase engagement, build relationships, and expand your reach on Instagram. Remember to tag relevant accounts and locations, use a mix of tags, limit tag use, and tag consistently to establish your brand's presence on Instagram.

PART 2

Content Strategy

CHAPTER 4

DEFINING YOUR TARGET AUDIENCE

IDENTIFYING YOUR IDEAL CUSTOMER AND THEIR NEEDS

The foundation of any successful Instagram marketing strategy rests on a deep understanding of your ideal customer. Often referred to as a "buyer persona," this detailed profile paints a clear picture of the individual you're striving to connect with. By pinpointing their demographics, interests, and online behavior, you can tailor your content and messaging to resonate with them on a deeper level, ultimately fostering brand loyalty and driving sales.

Demographics – The Foundation

Demographics provide a crucial starting point for understanding your ideal customer. Here's a breakdown of key demographic factors to consider:

- **Age:** Understanding your target audience's age range allows you to tailor your content and communication style accordingly. Younger demographics might respond well to humor and trendy visuals, while older audiences might prefer a more informative and straightforward approach.
- **Gender:** While some businesses cater to a unisex audience, many have a specific gender bias. Understanding the gender breakdown of your ideal customer base helps you curate content and messaging that resonates with their interests and preferences.
- **Location:** Are you targeting a local audience or aiming for global reach? Understanding your customer's geographic location influences factors like

content timing and cultural references utilized in your messaging.

- **Income and Education:** Consider the income level and educational background of your ideal customer. This awareness allows you to showcase your products or services in a way that aligns with their purchasing power and interests.
- **Occupation:** Understanding your target audience's profession can provide valuable insights into their lifestyle, needs, and pain points. This allows you to tailor your content to address challenges they might face in their professional lives. Utilize demographic data readily available from your existing customer base or conduct surveys to gain a clearer picture of your audience.

Psychographics – Beyond the Basics

Demographics offer a starting point, but to truly understand your ideal customer, you need to delve into their psychographics. These factors paint a picture of their:

- **Interests and Hobbies:** What are your ideal customers passionate about outside of your product or service? Understanding their interests allows you to create content that aligns with their hobbies and lifestyle, fostering a sense of connection.
- **Values and Beliefs:** What values and beliefs drive your ideal customer? Do they prioritize sustainability, social responsibility, or a sense of community? Aligning your brand messaging with their core values builds trust and loyalty.
- **Online Behavior:** Where does your ideal customer spend their time online? What social media platforms do they frequent? Knowing their online habits allows you to target them effectively across the digital landscape.

- **Challenges and Pain Points:** What are the challenges your ideal customer faces? What problems do your products or services solve? By understanding their pain points, you can position your brand as the solution they've been searching for. Conduct market research or leverage social listening tools to understand the online conversations and challenges your target audience is facing.

Putting the Pieces Together

Once you've gathered data on demographics and psychographics, it's time to create a comprehensive buyer persona. This detailed profile serves as a roadmap for your Instagram marketing strategy, ensuring your content resonates with your ideal customer. Here's how to construct your buyer persona:

- **Give Them a Name:** Assigning a name to your persona helps you visualize them as a real person, making it easier to understand their needs and motivations.
- **Craft a Narrative:** Weave together the demographic and psychographic information you've gathered to tell a story of your ideal customer. Describe their daily routine, challenges, and aspirations.
- **Identify Their Needs:** Clearly define the needs and desires your ideal customer has that your product or service can address.
- **Visualize Their Journey:** Map out the path your ideal customer takes when considering or purchasing your product or service. Where does Instagram fit into their decision-making process? Create multiple buyer personas if your business caters to diverse customer segments.

Tailoring Your Instagram Strategy

With a well-defined buyer persona in hand, you can now craft an Instagram strategy that resonates with your ideal customer. Here's how to translate your insights into action:

- **Content Creation:** Develop content that speaks directly to your ideal customer's interests, challenges, and aspirations.
- **Visual Style:** Curate a visual aesthetic that aligns with your target audience's preferences. Utilize colors, fonts, and editing styles that resonate with their sense of taste.
- **Messaging Tone:** Adjust your communication style to match your ideal customer's personality. A playful and humorous tone might work well for a younger audience, while a more professional and authoritative approach might be better suited for a business-oriented audience.

- **Hashtag Strategy:** Research and utilize hashtags that your ideal customer is likely to follow or search for. This ensures your content appears in relevant feeds and increases the chances of them discovering your brand.
- **Influencer Marketing:** Partner with influencers whose audience aligns with your ideal customer profile. This allows you to leverage their existing credibility and reach to connect with potential customers who already trust and respect their opinion.
- **Call to Actions:** Craft compelling calls to action (CTAs) within your captions and Stories. Whether it's encouraging them to visit your website, learn more about a product, or participate in a contest, make it clear what action you want your audience to take.

Remember: Understanding your ideal customer is an ongoing process. As you gather data and interact with your audience on Instagram, refine your buyer persona to ensure your content continues to resonate with their evolving needs and preferences. By consistently tailoring your Instagram strategy to your ideal customer, you'll build a loyal following, drive sales, and ultimately achieve your entrepreneurial goals.

CHAPTER 5

CREATING ENGAGING VISUAL CONTENT

UNDERSTANDING THE IMPORTANCE OF VISUAL CONTENT ON INSTAGRAM

Unlike its text-heavy counterparts, Instagram thrives on captivating imagery and videos that tell stories without a single word. For today's entrepreneur, mastering visual content is no longer an option, it's the cornerstone of a successful Instagram strategy. This chapter delves into the compelling reasons why visuals reign supreme on Instagram, equipping you with the knowledge and strategies to create content that stops the scroll, sparks engagement, and ultimately drives sales for your business.

Why Images and Videos Have an Advantage

Human brains are wired to process visuals significantly faster than text. Studies suggest that visual content is processed 60,000 times faster than text, making it a powerful tool to grab attention and leave a lasting impression on potential customers. Here's a deeper dive into the advantages visuals offer on Instagram:

- **Instantaneous Impact:** In the fast-paced world of social media, users are bombarded with content. A captivating image or video has the power to grab attention in a split second, piquing their curiosity and encouraging them to stop and engage with your post.
- **Emotional Connection:** Visuals have an unparalleled ability to evoke emotions. A well-crafted image or video can trigger feelings of joy, excitement, nostalgia, or even trust, fostering a deeper connection with your audience.

- **Storytelling Power:** Images and videos are natural storytellers. They allow you to showcase your products, services, or brand story in a more engaging and memorable way compared to text alone.
- **Brand Identity:** The visual elements you consistently use on Instagram, from color palettes to editing styles, contribute significantly to your brand identity. A cohesive visual aesthetic helps users instantly recognize your brand and understand its core values.
- **Increased Engagement:** Content that incorporates visuals consistently outperforms text-only posts. Images and videos encourage users to like, comment, and share your content, fostering a sense of community and propelling organic reach.

Functionality of Visual Content

While aesthetics are crucial, effective visual content on Instagram goes beyond just looking pretty. Here are some strategic ways to utilize visuals to achieve your business goals:

- **Product Showcase:** Instagram is a prime platform to showcase your products in a visually appealing way. Utilize high-quality photos and videos to highlight the features, benefits, and diverse applications of your offerings.
- **Lifestyle Integration:** Don't just showcase products in isolation. Create content that depicts your products seamlessly integrated into real-life situations. This allows potential customers to envision themselves using and benefiting from your offerings.
- **User-Generated Content (UGC):** Encourage customers to share their experiences with your brand using a specific branded hashtag. User-generated content fosters a sense of authenticity and social proof, building trust with potential customers.

- **Behind-the-Scenes Glimpses:** Offer viewers a peek into your company culture, production process, or team dynamics. This transparency humanizes your brand and fosters a sense of connection with your audience.
- **Informative Content:** Utilize visuals to create informative content like infographics, tutorials, or product demonstrations. This establishes you as a thought leader and educates potential customers about your offerings.

Strategic Considerations for Optimizing Visual Content for Success

Creating captivating visuals is just one step in the game. Here's how to optimize your visual content for maximum impact:

- **Captions that Complement:** While visuals grab attention, captions offer context and a call to action. Craft engaging captions that tell the story behind the image or video, highlight key features, and encourage users to take a desired action.
- **Strategic Hashtags:** Don't underestimate the power of hashtags! Research relevant hashtags your target audience uses and incorporate them strategically in your captions. This increases the discoverability of your content and broadens your reach.
- **Storytelling through Emojis:** Emojis can add personality and emotional depth to your captions. Use them strategically to emphasize key points, inject humor, or connect with your audience on a more informal level.
- **Accessibility Considerations:** Ensure your visual content is accessible to everyone. Utilize alt text descriptions for images to cater to visually impaired

users, and consider captions with clear audio descriptions for videos.

Building Engagement through Visuals

Visual content isn't just a one-way street. It's a powerful tool to foster engagement and build a thriving community around your brand. Here's how to leverage visuals to spark interaction:

- **Interactive Polls and Stickers:** Utilize Instagram's interactive tools like polls and question stickers within Stories and live sessions. Encourage viewers to participate in surveys and answer questions related to your products or services.
- **Contests and Giveaways:** Run visually-driven contests and giveaways that encourage user-generated content. Ask users to share photos or videos using a specific hashtag or incorporating your product in a creative way. This generates excitement, increases brand awareness, and fosters a sense of community.
- **Behind-the-Scenes Takeovers:** Invite brand ambassadors, influencers, or even loyal customers to take over your Instagram Stories for a day. Encourage them to share their experiences with your brand using a mix of photos and videos, offering a fresh perspective and engaging your audience in a new way.

Building a successful Instagram presence requires a commitment to high-quality visuals, a strategic approach to content creation, and continuous engagement with your audience. By mastering the art of visual storytelling and leveraging the platform's interactive features, you can transform your brand into a captivating force on Instagram, attracting new customers, fostering loyalty, and ultimately achieving your entrepreneurial goals.

TIPS FOR TAKING HIGH-QUALITY PHOTOS AND VIDEOS

While professional photography equipment can elevate your content, it's not always necessary. Today's smartphones boast impressive camera capabilities, and with a few key strategies, you can capture high-quality visuals that stop the scroll, showcase your brand story, and ultimately drive sales.

Lighting

Lighting is the foundation of any great photograph or video. Here's how to harness its power on Instagram:

- **Embrace Natural Light:** Whenever possible, utilize natural light for a soft and flattering effect. Early morning or late afternoon light (often referred to as "golden hour") offers a warm and inviting glow, perfect for showcasing products or capturing lifestyle content.
- **Diffuse Harsh Sunlight:** Avoid shooting directly under harsh midday sun, as it can create unflattering shadows and washed-out colors. Diffuse harsh sunlight with a sheer curtain or white sheet for a softer, more even light.
- **Artificial Light with Caution:** While artificial light can be helpful in controlled environments, use it cautiously. Incandescent bulbs can cast a yellow hue, while fluorescent lights can create a green tint. Experiment with different lighting setups and white balance settings on your camera app to achieve a natural look.
- Invest in a portable ring light for situations where natural light is limited. These affordable lighting tools offer diffused, adjustable lighting, perfect for product close-ups and flat lay photos.

Composition

Composition refers to the arrangement of elements within your frame. Here are some basic composition techniques to elevate your Instagram content:

- **Rule of Thirds:** Divide your frame into a 3x3 grid (either visually or using your camera app's grid overlay). Position your subject at one of the intersecting points for a more visually balanced and engaging composition.
- **Leading Lines:** Utilize natural lines within your environment to draw the viewer's eye towards your subject. This can be anything from a winding road to the edge of a table, creating a sense of depth and guiding the viewer's focus.
- **Negative Space:** Don't be afraid of empty space! Negative space can add balance and emphasize your subject. Experiment with different compositions to create a sense of simplicity and elegance.
- **Foreground, Midground, and Background:** Consider the layers within your frame. Utilize foreground elements to frame your subject and create depth. Ensure the background complements your subject without distracting from it.
- Experiment with different camera angles! Don't just stick to eye level shots. Explore high angle, low angle, or close-up perspectives to add variety and visual interest to your content.

Capturing Sharp Images

Camera shake can ruin an otherwise perfect shot. Here are some tips to ensure sharp and crisp photos and videos:

- **Utilize a Tripod (Optional):** For ultimate stability, especially in low-light situations, consider using a

tripod. Even a small, portable tripod can make a significant difference in image quality.
- **The Two-Second Rule:** When shooting handheld, hold your breath and press the shutter button for a brief pause, minimizing camera shake. This "two-second rule" helps ensure sharper images.
- **Burst Mode:** Utilize your camera app's burst mode function, which captures several photos in rapid succession. This increases your chances of capturing a sharp image, especially when photographing moving subjects.
- If you're using a tripod, consider utilizing a remote shutter release button. This allows you to trigger the camera without touching it, further minimizing camera shake.

Highlighting Your Subject

A clear and well-focused subject is crucial for captivating photos and videos. Here's how to master focus on your smartphone camera:

- **Tap to Focus:** Most smartphone cameras allow you to tap on the screen to designate a specific focus point. Tap on the area you want the camera to focus on before capturing your photo or video.
- **Object Tracking:** Many newer smartphone camera apps offer object tracking features. Simply tap and hold on your subject, and the camera will automatically keep it in focus, even if it's moving. This is particularly helpful for capturing action shots or product demonstrations.
- **Manual Focus (Optional):** Some advanced smartphone camera apps offer manual focus capabilities. While this requires practice, it allows you for ultimate control over the focus point within your frame.

- Pay attention to the depth of field. A shallow depth of field (where only your subject is in focus and the background is blurred) can create a dramatic effect and draw attention to your product. Experiment with different focus settings to achieve the desired visual impact.

Editing Essentials for Enhancing Your Visuals

While smartphone cameras are increasingly sophisticated, basic editing can elevate your photos and videos to a professional level. Here are some key editing considerations:

- **Exposure and Brightness:** Adjust the exposure and brightness to ensure your visuals aren't too dark or washed out. Aim for a balanced and natural look.
- **Contrast and Saturation:** Play with contrast and saturation to enhance the vibrancy and depth of your visuals. However, avoid overdoing it, as excessive adjustments can create an unnatural look.
- **Sharpening:** Sharpening can add a touch of crispness to your visuals. Use this tool subtly to avoid creating a grainy or overly processed image.
- **Cropping and Straightening:** Utilize cropping tools to adjust the composition of your image and straighten any tilted horizons.
- **Presets and Filters (Use with Caution):** Many editing apps offer pre-set filters or editing styles. While these can be a time-saver, use them cautiously. Ensure the chosen filter complements your brand aesthetic and doesn't overpower the natural beauty of your visuals.
- Utilize a consistent editing style across your Instagram profile. This creates a cohesive visual identity and makes your brand instantly recognizable to your audience.

Capturing Engaging Video Content

While photos are a mainstay of Instagram, captivating videos can truly grab attention and tell a compelling story. Here's how to capture engaging video content for your business:

- **Planning and Scripting (Optional):** For longer videos, consider creating a brief storyboard or script to ensure a clear narrative flow. However, don't be afraid to experiment with spontaneous and creative video content as well.
- **Stabilization Features:** Many smartphone camera apps offer built-in stabilization features that can significantly reduce shakiness in your videos. Utilize them for smoother and more professional-looking footage.
- **Sound Matters:** Pay attention to the audio quality of your videos. Invest in a directional microphone attachment for your smartphone, especially if you're planning to capture interviews or product demonstrations in noisy environments.
- **Music and Sound Effects:** Strategic use of music and sound effects can enhance the emotional impact and storytelling power of your videos. However, be mindful of copyright restrictions and ensure any music you use is licensed for commercial use.
- Utilize Instagram Reels for short-form video content. Explore creative editing tools, music overlays, and text effects to create engaging and trendy video clips that capture attention within the first few seconds.

Additional Tips

Remember, capturing high-quality visuals is just the first step. Here are some final tips to ensure your photos and videos resonate with your target audience:

- **Know Your Audience:** Tailor your visuals to your target audience's preferences. Consider the types of visuals they're likely to find engaging and that align with your brand identity.
- **Consistency is Key:** Maintain a consistent visual aesthetic across your profile. This includes utilizing similar color palettes, editing styles, and visual elements to create a recognizable brand identity.
- **Post Regularly:** Develop a content calendar and post high-quality visuals regularly to maintain audience engagement and keep your brand top-of-mind.
- **Engage with Your Audience:** Respond to comments, answer questions, and participate in conversations around your visuals. This fosters a sense of community and builds relationships with your audience.

By mastering these tips and consistently creating captivating visual content, you can transform your Instagram presence from static and unremarkable to a vibrant and engaging hub that attracts new customers, fosters brand loyalty, and ultimately propels your entrepreneurial journey towards success.

EDITING AND CAPTIONING YOUR VISUAL CONTENT

To truly resonate with your audience and drive engagement, you need to refine and polish your content with strategic editing and compelling captions.

Mastering the Art of Enhancement

Smartphone editing tools have come a long way, offering an array of features to transform your photos and videos from good to great. Here's a breakdown of key editing techniques for Instagram success:

- **Exposure and Brightness:** A well-exposed image is essential. Adjust the exposure to ensure your visuals aren't too dark or washed out. Aim for a balanced and natural look, but don't be afraid to experiment with a high-contrast or light-and-airy edit depending on your desired visual style.
- **Contrast and Saturation:** Play with contrast and saturation to enhance the vibrancy and depth of your visuals. Increased contrast can create a more dramatic effect, while boosting saturation can make colors pop. However, avoid overdoing it, as excessive adjustments can create an unnatural look.
- **Highlights and Shadows:** Many editing tools allow you to adjust highlights and shadows independently. This offers granular control over the brightness and darkness within your image. Use this technique to add depth and dimension to your photos, particularly for product close-ups.
- **Sharpening and Clarity:** Sharpening can add a touch of crispness to your visuals, while clarity can enhance details and textures. Use these tools subtly to avoid creating a grainy or overly processed image.
- **Cropping and Straightening:** Utilize cropping tools to adjust the composition of your image and straighten any tilted horizons. A well-composed image creates a sense of balance and professionalism.

Tip: Utilize a consistent editing style across your Instagram profile. This creates a cohesive visual identity and makes your brand instantly recognizable to your audience. Consider creating a set of pre-sets within your editing app to streamline the process and maintain consistent color palettes and editing styles.

Advanced Editing Techniques

While the core editing tools mentioned above are essential, several advanced techniques can elevate your visuals further:

- **Selective Adjustments:** Many advanced editing apps allow you to make adjustments to specific areas of your image. This allows you to selectively brighten a product in a photo or darken the background to make your subject stand out.
- **Color Correction:** Utilize color correction tools to fine-tune the color balance of your images. This can be particularly helpful when dealing with artificial lighting or inconsistent color temperatures.
- **Noise Reduction:** In low-light situations, photos can appear grainy due to noise. Utilize noise reduction tools to smooth out the image and create a cleaner look. However, be careful not to over-apply noise reduction, as it can blur details.
- **Local Adjustments:** Some editing apps offer functionalities like dodging and burning, which allow you to lighten or darken specific areas of your image. This technique can be used to draw attention to specific elements or create a vignette effect.

Tip: Experiment with different editing techniques! Mastering advanced tools can give you creative freedom and allow you to create unique and eye-catching visuals for your brand. However, don't be afraid to keep it simple – focus on enhancing the natural beauty of your visuals rather than creating an overly processed look.

By mastering the art of editing, you can transform your Instagram visuals from static images into captivating stories that resonate with your target audience. Remember, consistency is key. Regularly posting high-quality visuals, accompanied by well-written captions, fuels audience engagement, expands your reach, and ultimately drives sales for your business. With dedication and these valuable tools in your arsenal, you can harness the power of Instagram to propel your entrepreneurial journey forward.

CHAPTER 6

CRAFTING EFFECTIVE CAPTIONS AND CTAS

WRITING ENGAGING AND INFORMATIVE CAPTIONS

A well-written caption tells a story, sparks conversation, and ultimately compels your audience to take action. When you are able to learn how to successfully craft engaging and informative captions, you will have unlocked the key to transforming casual viewers into loyal brand advocates; pushing your brand forward and increasing the success of your business.

Captivating Your Audience

Forget simple descriptions of your photos and videos. Engaging captions weave a narrative around your visuals, drawing viewers in and fostering a deeper connection with your brand.

Help your audience connect with the deeper meaning behind your visuals. Ask yourself: What emotions does the image evoke? What lifestyle or value does it represent?

Consider creating relatable characters within your captions. These could be satisfied customers using your product, team members showcasing your company culture, or even fictional personas embodying your brand values. Characters inject personality, make your content more engaging, and allow viewers to form emotional connections.

Frame your content around a problem your target audience faces and how your brand offers the solution. For example, if you sell eco-friendly cleaning products, your caption could tell the story of a busy parent struggling to keep a clean home without harsh chemicals. Highlight how your products provide a safe and effective solution.

Don't just tell your audience what you do, tell them why it matters. Explain the purpose behind your brand, the inspiration for your products, or the impact your business creates. Connecting with your audience on a deeper level fosters loyalty and trust.

Pro Tip: Utilize questions within your captions to spark conversation, encourage engagement, and gain valuable insights into your target market. Ask your audience about their experiences, preferences, or opinions.

Educating Your Audience

While storytelling is captivating, informative captions offer valuable knowledge and insights to your audience. This establishes you as a thought leader in your industry and positions your brand as a trusted resource.

Offer viewers a peek into the inner workings of your business with behind-the-scenes glimpses. Share how your products are made, introduce your team members, or showcase your company culture. This level of transparency fosters trust and humanizes your brand.

Share your expertise with your audience. Post informative captions about trends in your industry, tips and tricks related to your products or services, or answer frequently asked questions. This positions you as a valuable resource and demonstrates your commitment to customer education.

Don't just showcase your products; explain their unique features and the benefits they offer to your target audience. Focus on how your products solve problems, improve lives, or enhance user experiences.

Utilize Instagram's caption space to educate your audience about topics relevant to your brand. This could involve sharing infographics, short tutorials, or even quick "how-to" guides. Educational content establishes you as an authority and provides valuable information to your followers.

Pro Tip: Utilize statistics and data to support your claims in informative captions. Statistics add credibility and showcase the effectiveness of your products or services.

Engaging with Your Audience

Captions aren't one-way streets. To truly harness their power, foster interaction with your audience. Here are some strategies to encourage engagement:

- **Respond to Comments:** Don't leave comments hanging. Respond promptly, answer questions, and engage in genuine conversation. This builds relationships, fosters a sense of community, and shows your audience you care.
- **Run Contests and Giveaways:** Who doesn't love a chance to win? Host contests and giveaways with clear participation guidelines and attractive prizes. This is a fun way to generate excitement, increase brand awareness, and attract new followers.
- **Encourage User-Generated Content (UGC):** Turn your audience into brand ambassadors. Encourage them to create content related to your brand using a specific hashtag. This leverages the power of social proof, increases brand reach, and showcases the

value your products or services offer through real-world examples.

- **Collaborate with Influencers:** Partner with relevant influencers in your niche. Utilize their reach and established audience to promote your brand through engaging captions and visuals. However, choose influencers who genuinely align with your brand values for authenticity.

Consistency is key. Regularly posting high-quality visuals accompanied by well-written captions is crucial for sustained audience engagement and brand growth. By mastering the art of storytelling, crafting informative content, and strategically incorporating calls to action, you can transform your Instagram captions from mere text blurbs into powerful tools that drive engagement, build brand loyalty, and ultimately propel your business forward.

USING CALLS-TO-ACTION (CTAS) TO DRIVE WEBSITE TRAFFIC AND SALES

At the end of the day, beyond the monetization of your account, the ultimate goal of making use of Instagram for business is to convert casual viewers into loyal customers. This is where the power of the Call to Action (CTA) comes into play. A well-crafted CTA within your caption strategically directs your audience towards a desired action, ultimately driving website traffic, boosting sales, and propelling your business forward.

Defining Your Desired Action

Before crafting your CTA, clearly define the specific action you want your audience to take after viewing your post. Here are some common goals for Instagram CTAs:

- **Drive Website Traffic:** Direct viewers to visit your website for more information about your products, services, or brand story.
- **Boost Sales:** Encourage viewers to purchase a product directly through your website or a linked online store.
- **Increase Engagement:** Prompt viewers to like your post, leave a comment, or participate in a contest or giveaway.
- **Grow Your Following:** Instruct viewers to follow your account for more engaging content and brand updates.
- **Download Content:** Encourage viewers to download a free resource, such as an ebook, infographic, or discount code.

By clearly defining your desired action, you can craft a CTA that is specific, actionable, and most importantly, effective.

Crafting Enticing CTAs

The wording of your CTA plays a crucial role in its success. Here are some strategies to craft CTAs that entice your audience to take action:

- **Action Verbs:** Utilize strong action verbs that leave no room for ambiguity. Words like "Shop Now," "Learn More," "Download Here," or "Click the Link in Bio" are clear and direct, prompting viewers towards the desired action.
- **Sense of Urgency:** Sometimes, a gentle nudge can encourage viewers to act. Phrases like "Limited Time Offer," "Shop Before They're Gone," or "Download Today" create a sense of urgency, motivating viewers to take advantage of the opportunity before it disappears.
- **Benefit-Driven Language:** Focus on the benefits your audience will receive by taking action. Instead of

simply saying "Visit Our Website," highlight the value proposition – "Visit Our Website to Discover How We Can Help You Achieve Your Fitness Goals."

- **Keep it Short and Sweet:** In the fast-paced world of Instagram, brevity is key. Aim for concise CTAs that are easy to understand and remember.

Tip: Utilize emojis strategically within your CTA. Emojis can add a touch of personality, visually highlight your call to action, and make your caption more visually appealing. However, avoid overusing them, as it can make your CTA appear unprofessional.

Optimizing Your CTA Placement

Strategic placement of your CTA within your caption can significantly impact its effectiveness. Here's how to optimize your CTA placement:

- **Early and Often:** Don't wait until the end of your caption to include your CTA. Repeat it strategically throughout the caption, particularly after sparking interest with your visuals and storytelling.
- **Question Prompts:** End your caption with a compelling question that naturally leads into your CTA. For example, "Ready to take your travel photography to the next level? Download our free guide today!"
- **Utilize Bio Link:** Instagram allows you to include a clickable link in your bio. This is a prime location to showcase your primary CTA, such as directing viewers to your website or a specific product landing page. Update your bio link regularly to reflect your current marketing focus.

Tip: Track the performance of your CTAs using Instagram Insights. This valuable data reveals which CTAs resonate most with your audience, allowing you to refine your strategy for future posts.

A/B Testing

The world of marketing thrives on experimentation. A/B testing allows you to compare different versions of your CTAs to see which ones perform best. Here's how to leverage A/B testing for your Instagram CTAs:

- **Test Different Wording:** Create two captions with identical visuals but slightly different CTA wording. Track which version receives a higher click-through rate to determine the most effective wording.
- **Highlight Incentives:** Test the impact of offering incentives within your CTAs. Compare a CTA with a discount code to one without to see if the incentive drives higher engagement.
- **Placement and Timing:** Experiment with placing your CTA at the beginning, middle, or end of your caption. Additionally, test posting at different times of day to see when your audience is most receptive to your CTAs.

BEST PRACTICES FOR CAPTION LENGTH, TONE, AND STYLE

A well-crafted caption acts as a bridge between your visuals and your audience, fostering connection, sparking conversation, and ultimately driving action. The goal is to craft captions that are not only informative and engaging but also optimized for length, tone, and style to resonate with your target audience and propel your brand forward.

Finding the Sweet Spot in Caption Length

There's no one-size-fits-all answer to the ideal caption length on Instagram. The optimal word count depends on several factors, including the complexity of your message, the type of visual you're posting, and the desired audience response. Here's a breakdown to guide your decision-making:

- **Short and Sweet (Under 100 Words):** Ideal for quick announcements, product teasers, or behind-the-scenes glimpses. Short captions are easily digestible and well-suited for posts featuring strong visuals that speak for themselves.
- **Engaging Narrative (100-250 Words):** This range allows you to weave a captivating story around your visuals. Share a customer testimonial, highlight the inspiration behind your product, or offer quick tips or tricks related to your brand.
- **In-Depth Explanations (250+ Words):** Use longer captions for educational content, industry insights, or detailed product descriptions. Break down complex topics into digestible chunks, utilize bullet points or numbered lists for easy reading, and consider incorporating visuals like infographics to enhance understanding.

Tip: Regardless of length, avoid large blocks of text. Utilize line breaks and emojis strategically to improve readability on mobile screens.

Establishing Brand Tone

The tone of your captions is the voice of your brand. It reflects your personality, values, and how you want to connect with your audience. Here are some factors to consider when establishing your brand tone:

- **Target Audience:** Who are you trying to reach? Understanding your ideal customer's demographics, interests, and preferred communication style helps you tailor your tone accordingly.
- **Brand Personality:** What are the core values and personality traits you want your brand to embody? Are you playful and humorous, professional and authoritative, or something in between?
- **Content Type:** The tone might vary slightly depending on the type of content you're posting. A product announcement might have a more promotional tone, while a behind-the-scenes glimpse could be lighthearted and conversational.

Examples of Brand Tone:

- **Informative and Authoritative:** "As a leading provider of sustainable cleaning solutions, we're committed to..."
- **Playful and Engaging:** "Looking for a laugh? Check out our latest product that will make cleaning a breeze!"
- **Inspirational and Uplifting:** "Empower yourself to achieve your goals. Let us show you how..."

By establishing a consistent brand tone, you build brand recognition and trust with your audience. They'll come to recognize and appreciate your unique voice, fostering a stronger connection with your brand.

Maintaining Cohesion and Consistency

Beyond tone, your caption style encompasses the overall aesthetic and approach you take to crafting your messages. Here are some strategies to establish a cohesive and consistent style:

- **Word Choice:** Utilize language that aligns with your brand voice. Maintain a professional tone for a B2B brand, or incorporate a conversational style for a B2C audience.
- **Visual Language:** Consider how your caption's language complements your visuals. Does your caption use descriptive language to evoke emotions, or is it concise and factual, allowing the visuals to tell the story?
- **Hashtags:** Utilize a consistent mix of relevant hashtags to categorize your content and increase discoverability. Explore branded hashtags, industry-specific hashtags, and popular trending hashtags to optimize your reach.
- **Storytelling:** Storytelling is a powerful tool for captivating your audience. Weave narratives into your captions, even for product-focused posts. Highlight how your product solves a problem, enhances a lifestyle, or creates a positive impact.

Tip: Develop a content calendar that outlines your posting schedule and the general style of captions for each post. This ensures consistency and streamlines your content creation process.

By mastering the art of caption length, tone, and style, you can transform your Instagram presence from a collection of random posts into a strategically crafted narrative that resonates with your audience. Remember, consistency is key. Regularly posting high-quality visuals accompanied by well-written captions that reflect your brand voice and style fosters engagement, builds trust, and ultimately fuels your brand's growth and success on Instagram.

CHAPTER 7
CONTENT CALENDAR AND PLANNING

UNDERSTANDING THE IMPORTANCE OF A CONTENT CALENDAR

Understanding the importance of a content calendar is crucial for businesses on Instagram. A content calendar is a strategic plan that outlines your content strategy, including the type of content, posting schedule, and goals for each post.

A content calendar offers numerous benefits, including consistency, organization, time-saving, and goal-oriented content. It ensures consistent posting, which is essential for building audience engagement and trust. It also helps you organize your content strategy, ensuring that you're always prepared and never miss a posting opportunity.

Additionally, a content calendar saves time by allowing you to plan and schedule content in advance. Most importantly, it helps you align your content strategy with your business goals, ensuring that every post is purposeful and effective.

A content calendar typically includes the content type, posting schedule, content goals, target audience, and hashtags. To create a content calendar, define your content strategy, choose a scheduling tool, plan your content, and schedule your content in advance.

It's essential to plan ahead, scheduling content at least a week in advance to ensure consistency and organization. Varying content types keeps your audience engaged and interested. Research and use relevant hashtags to increase visibility and engagement. Tracking your content performance and adjusting your strategy accordingly is also crucial.

By understanding the importance of a content calendar and implementing one for your business, you'll be able to create a strategic content strategy that drives engagement, increases brand awareness, and ultimately commercializes your Instagram presence.

TOOLS AND APPS FOR CONTENT PLANNING AND SCHEDULING

In today's fast-paced digital landscape, staying ahead of the curve on Instagram requires careful planning and scheduling of content. As an entrepreneur seeking to commercialize your Instagram presence, leveraging the right tools and apps can make all the difference. In this section, we'll delve into the world of content planning and scheduling, exploring the top tools and apps that can help you streamline your strategy and drive business results.

Content planning and scheduling are crucial aspects of any successful Instagram marketing strategy. By planning and scheduling your content in advance, you can ensure consistency, save time, and align your content with your business goals. However, with the plethora of tools and apps available, it can be overwhelming to determine which ones are best suited for your needs.

First and foremost, let's discuss the importance of content planning and scheduling. Consistency is key to building trust and engagement with your audience. By planning and scheduling your content, you can ensure that your posts are regular, timely, and aligned with your business objectives. Moreover, content planning and scheduling can help you save time, allowing you to focus on other aspects of your business. With the right tools and apps, you can automate the process, ensuring that your content is published even when you're not actively online.

So, which tools and apps should you consider? Let's start with Statusbrew, a comprehensive platform that guides you from content research to final execution. With Statusbrew, you can keep track of topics that interest you, curate content on Twitter and Instagram, and engage in conversations where you're mentioned. Moreover, you can schedule your content in advance, ensuring that your posts are published at the right time to maximize engagement.

Another tool worth considering is Surfer SEO, a user-friendly platform designed to assist in creating content strategies that perform well in search engine rankings. With Surfer SEO, you can conduct SEO audits, keep an eye on your search engine results page positions, and create groups of related keywords to build your authority in your field. The content planner feature automatically suggests new content topics and keywords, making it easier to develop a robust content strategy.

Ahrefs is another popular tool that offers a content planning feature to simplify content management. With Ahrefs, you can identify trending topics and popular content, conduct thorough SEO audits, and analyze your website's progress in search engine rankings. The content explorer feature allows you to dive into detailed keyword research, enabling you to fine-tune your approach and create content that resonates with your audience.

Trello is a straightforward project management tool that's perfect for organizing your content creation process. With Trello, you can make lists, set up to-do tasks, and prioritize your workflow. The collaborative nature of Trello makes it an excellent choice for teams, allowing multiple people to work together on content projects. Moreover, Trello integrates with platforms like Slack and Jira, making it easier to streamline your workflow.

Notion is another app that's perfect for streamlining your digital and content creation tasks. With Notion, you can quickly capture and organize notes, create checklists or detailed project boards, and even create wikis. The real-time collaboration feature allows you to work with your team seamlessly, making it easier to manage projects and brainstorm ideas.

Canva is a user-friendly graphic design tool that's perfect for creating visuals such as posters, flyers, marketing materials, and social media posts. The content planner feature in Canva Pro allows you to create and schedule posts for platforms like Facebook, Twitter, Instagram, Pinterest, and LinkedIn on a daily, weekly, or monthly basis. With Canva, you can choose from a vast selection of customizable social media templates, collaborate with your team in real-time, and directly schedule your posts to your social media channels.

Google Docs and Google Sheets are free tools which are great for collaboration and creating an editorial calendar. Google Docs allows you to create and manage top-notch content, while Google Sheets is perfect for creating a content calendar to keep your content organized and on track.

Google Calendar is an online scheduling tool that simplifies planning your workflow. It's packed with features, including scheduling meetings, accessing your schedule on mobile, and getting reminders for upcoming activities.

Asana is a tool that is designed for managing projects and organizing work. It allows your team to collaborate on a single platform, offers various project views, and automates many routine tasks. It supports over 200 integrations to enhance your ability to manage content projects.

In addition to these tools, there are many other apps and platforms available to help you plan and schedule your content. Some popular options include CoSchedule, Feedly,

Airtable, Tweetdeck, Planable, Sked Social, Post Planner, StatusBrew, MeetEdgar, eClincher, and NapoleonCat.

When choosing a tool or app for content planning and scheduling, consider the following factors:

- Functionality: Some tools are simple and require manual posting, while others are more advanced and automate posting.
- Features: Ensure the tool offers the features you need, such as managing multiple social media accounts or team collaboration.
- Customizations: Choose a tool that allows customization of the calendar layout, categories, and tags to fit your needs.
- Ease of use: Opt for a user-friendly tool with an intuitive interface.
- Cost: Select a tool that fits your budget and offers the necessary features.

Some popular tools for content planning and scheduling include:

- HubSpot's Social Media Calendar Template (free)
- HubSpot Social Media Management Software (free tools available, paid plans start at $20/mo/seat)
- Google Drive (free for personal use, Google Workspace plans for businesses start at $6 per month)
- Jotform Social Media Calendar (template available)
- Firefly Marketing Social Media Content Calendar (template available)

Remember to consider your specific needs and budget when selecting a tool.

PART 3

Advertising and Promotion

CHAPTER 8X

SETTING UP YOUR INSTAGRAM ADS ACCOUNT

CREATING AN INSTAGRAM ADS ACCOUNT AND SETTING UP YOUR PAYMENT METHOD

Creating an Instagram Ads account is a crucial step in commercializing your Instagram presence. With Instagram Ads, you can reach a larger audience, drive website traffic, and generate sales. In this section, we'll delve into the details of creating an Instagram Ads account and setting up your payment method, providing you with a comprehensive guide to help you commercialize your Instagram presence.

To create an Instagram Ads account, follow these steps:

- Log in to your Instagram account
- Tap the three horizontal lines on the top-right corner
- Tap "Settings"
- Tap "Business"
- Tap "Advertise"
- Tap "Create an Ad Account"

Fill in the required information, including your business name, email address, and password. You'll also need to provide your business address and tax identification number.

Setting Up Your Payment Method
Once you've created your Instagram Ads account, you'll need to set up your payment method. Instagram Ads accepts various payment methods, including credit cards, debit cards, and PayPal.
To set up your payment method:

- Log in to your Instagram Ads account
- Tap the three horizontal lines on the top-right corner

- Tap "Settings"
- Tap "Payment Methods"
- Tap "Add Payment Method"

Enter your payment information, including your card number, expiration date, and security code. You'll also need to provide your billing address.

Tips for Creating an Instagram Ads Account and Setting Up Your Payment Method

- Use a business email address to create your Instagram Ads account
- Ensure your business address and tax identification number are accurate
- Use a secure payment method, such as a credit card or PayPal
- Keep your payment information up to date to avoid any disruptions in your ad campaigns

UNDERSTANDING AD OBJECTIVES AND TARGETING OPTIONS

Understanding ad objectives and targeting options is crucial for creating effective Instagram ad campaigns. With Instagram's robust advertising platform, you can reach your target audience, drive website traffic, generate sales, and build brand awareness.

Ad objectives are the goals you want to achieve with your ad campaign. Instagram offers various ad objectives, including awareness, consideration, and conversion. Awareness objectives help you reach new audiences and build brand awareness.

Consideration objectives drive website traffic, increase engagement, and generate leads. Conversion objectives drive sales, sign-ups, and other conversions. When selecting an ad objective, consider your business goals and what you want to achieve with your ad campaign.

Targeting options are used to reach your target audience. Instagram offers robust targeting options, including demographics, interests, behaviors, connections, and lookalike audiences. Demographics targeting allows you to target users based on age, gender, location, language, and occupation. Interests targeting allows you to target users based on their hobbies, passions, and interests.

Behaviors targeting allows you to target users based on their purchase behavior, browsing behavior, and device usage. Connections targeting allows you to target users who are connected to your page or have engaged with your content. Lookalike audiences targeting allows you to target users who are similar to your existing audience.

It's important to align your ad objective with your business goal. If you want to drive sales, select the conversion objective. If you want to build brand awareness, select the awareness objective. Use targeting options to reach your ideal audience. For example, if you're a fashion brand, target users who are interested in fashion and have purchased fashion items online.

Lookalike audiences are a powerful targeting option that allows you to target users who are similar to your existing audience. This can help you expand your reach and target users who are likely to be interested in your brand. Custom audiences allow you to target users who have engaged with your content or visited your website. This can help you target users who are already familiar with your brand and are more likely to convert.

Continuously monitoring and optimizing your ad campaigns is crucial to ensure they are performing well and achieving your business goals. Use Instagram's built-in analytics tool to track your ad performance and make adjustments as needed.

By understanding ad objectives and targeting options, you'll be able to create effective Instagram ad campaigns that drive business results. Remember to align your ad objective with your business goal, use targeting options to reach your ideal audience, use lookalike audiences to expand your reach, use custom audiences to target engaged users, and continuously monitor and optimize your ad campaigns.

CREATING YOUR FIRST AD

Once you've set up your ad account, it's time to create your first ad. Follow these steps:

- Tap the "Create Ad" button
- Select your ad objective (awareness, consideration, or conversion)
- Upload your ad creative (image or video)
- Enter your ad copy (headline, description, and call-to-action)
- Select your target audience (using targeting options such as demographics, interests, and behaviors)
- Set your budget and bid strategy
- Review and confirm your ad settings

Tips for Creating Your First Ad

- Use a business email address to create your ad account
- Ensure your business address and tax identification number are accurate
- Use high-quality ad creative that aligns with your brand
- Keep your ad copy concise and clear
- Target your ideal audience using targeting options

- Start with a small budget and test your ad performance

CHAPTER 9

CREATING EFFECTIVE AD CONTENT

UNDERSTANDING THE IMPORTANCE OF EYE-CATCHING AD CREATIVE

In the ever-churning feed of Instagram, attention spans are fleeting. Captivating visuals are the currency of engagement, and within the realm of Instagram advertising, effective ad creatives are the golden ticket to success. This chapter equips you with the knowledge and strategies to craft eye-catching ad creatives that pierce through the noise, grab attention, and propel your brand towards its advertising goals.

Understanding how users interact with content on Instagram is crucial before diving into creative strategies. Users spend an average of less than three seconds per Instagram post, highlighting the need for visuals that instantly capture attention and spark curiosity. Humans are wired to respond to emotions. Effective ad creatives evoke feelings of joy, excitement, curiosity, or even nostalgia, prompting users to stop scrolling and engage with your ad. Visuals are a universal language. A powerful image or captivating video can tell a story in a split second, bypassing the need for lengthy text explanations and resonating with a broader audience.

High-quality visuals are the cornerstone of eye-catching ad creatives. Utilize high-resolution, visually appealing images that showcase your products, services, or brand aesthetic. Experiment with compositions, color palettes, and lighting to create a distinctive visual style. Incorporate captivating graphic design elements to enhance your images. Bold text overlays, creative typography, or eye-catching illustrations can make your ad stand out. Leverage short-form video formats like Instagram Reels or Stories to showcase product demonstrations, customer testimonials, or behind-the-scenes glimpses of your brand. While professional visuals are important, consider incorporating user-generated content (UGC) into your ad campaigns. UGC fosters trust and relatability, showcasing how real people interact with your brand.

Static visuals are essential, but incorporating motion and sound can elevate your ad creatives. Animated elements, like product demonstrations or explainer videos, can add a dynamic touch to your ads and enhance user engagement. Utilize creative transitions between scenes in your videos to keep viewers glued to the screen. Sound effects and music can add emotional depth and enhance the overall storytelling experience within your video ads. Not all platforms support sound by default, so utilize eye-catching visuals and clear captions to ensure your message resonates even with the sound muted.

Effective ad creatives go beyond simply showcasing your product. They tell a compelling story that resonates with your target audience. Evoke feelings of happiness, excitement, aspiration, or nostalgia. Connect your brand with a positive emotional response that viewers will associate with your product or service. Don't just list product specifications. Show how your product solves a problem, enhances a lifestyle, or fulfills a desire. Consider incorporating relatable characters into your ad narratives. This could be a satisfied customer using your product, a team member showcasing your brand culture, or even an animated persona embodying your brand values. Characters inject personality and make your ad content more engaging. Frame your ad around a problem your target audience faces and showcase how your brand offers the solution. Leave viewers wanting more. Don't reveal everything in your ad. Spark curiosity and encourage viewers to learn more about your brand by visiting your landing page or website.

The world of marketing thrives on experimentation. A/B testing allows you to compare different versions of your ad creatives to see which ones resonate most effectively with your target audience. Test different visual formats, headline copy, calls to action, and even your target audience itself to identify the segments that convert best for your brand. By embracing A/B testing and iteratively refining your ad creatives, you can significantly improve campaign performance, maximize your return on investment (ROI), and achieve your advertising goals on Instagram.

Effective measurement and analysis are crucial for understanding campaign performance and refining your strategy for future success. Track key metrics like impressions, reach, click-through rate (CTR), engagement rate, and conversions. By analyzing these metrics, you can identify which ad creatives resonate best with your audience and which elements drive the most conversions. Utilize Instagram's built-in analytics tools or integrate your ad campaigns with external analytics platforms to gain deeper insights into audience behavior and campaign performance.

Crafting eye-catching ad creatives is an art form. With a solid understanding of user behavior, the power of visuals and storytelling, and the strategic application of A/B testing and data analysis, you can transform your Instagram advertising efforts from a guessing game into a well-oiled machine for driving brand awareness, engagement, and ultimately, sales success. Remember, consistency is key. Regularly experiment, analyze, and refine your approach to create ad creatives that not only grab attention but also resonate with your target audience and propel your brand towards achieving its Instagram advertising goals.

CHAPTER 9

TARGETING AND BUDGETING FOR ADS

UNDERSTANDING INSTAGRAM'S TARGETING OPTIONS

Instagram's targeting options are a powerful tool for businesses looking to reach their ideal audience. With demographics, interests, and behaviors targeting, you can ensure that your ads are seen by the people who matter most to your business.

Demographics targeting allows you to target users based on their age, gender, location, language, and occupation. This targeting option is ideal for businesses that want to reach a specific age group, gender, or location. For example, a fashion brand targeting women aged 25-45 living in urban areas.

Interests targeting allows you to target users based on their hobbies, passions, and interests. This targeting option is ideal for businesses that want to reach users who are interested in specific topics or activities. For example, a travel brand targeting users who are interested in travel, adventure, and culture.

Behaviors targeting allows you to target users based on their purchase behavior, browsing behavior, and device usage. This targeting option is ideal for businesses that want to reach users who have shown specific behaviors online. For example, a beauty brand targeting users who have purchased beauty products online in the past.

Using a combination of targeting options allows you to reach your ideal audience with precision. Continuously monitoring and optimizing your targeting options ensures maximum ROI. By understanding and utilizing Instagram's targeting options, you'll be able to reach your ideal audience, drive business results, and commercialize your Instagram presence.

Not using targeting options effectively can lead to wasted ad spend and poor ad performance. Not monitoring and optimizing targeting options can lead to missed opportunities and poor ROI. Not using a combination of targeting options can lead to a limited reach and poor ad performance. Not targeting the right audience can lead to poor engagement and poor ad performance. Not continuously tracking and measuring ad performance can lead to missed opportunities and poor ROI.

By understanding and utilizing Instagram's targeting options, you'll be able to reach your ideal audience, drive business results, and commercialize your Instagram presence.

SETTING A BUDGET FOR YOUR AD CAMPAIGNS

Setting a budget for your ad campaigns is a crucial step in commercializing your Instagram presence. With a well-planned budget, you can ensure that your ads reach the right audience, drive website traffic, generate sales, and build brand awareness. In this section, we'll delve into the details of setting a budget for your ad campaigns, providing you with a comprehensive guide to help you commercialize your Instagram presence.

Determining Your Ad Budget

Determining your ad budget requires careful consideration of several factors, including your business goals, target audience, ad objectives, and industry benchmarks. Start by defining your business goals and what you want to achieve with your ad campaigns. Are you looking to drive website traffic, generate sales, or build brand awareness? Next, consider your target audience and their demographics, interests, and behaviors. Understanding your target audience will help you determine how much to budget for ad spend.

Ad Objectives and Budget

Your ad objectives play a significant role in determining your ad budget. Instagram offers various ad objectives, including awareness, consideration, and conversion. Awareness objectives require a higher budget to reach a larger audience, while consideration and conversion objectives require a lower budget to target users who are already familiar with your brand.

Industry Benchmarks and Budget

Industry benchmarks provide valuable insights into how much businesses in your industry are spending on ad campaigns. Research industry benchmarks to determine how much to budget for ad spend. For example, if you're in the fashion industry, you may need to budget more for ad spend due to high competition.

Setting a Daily or Lifetime Budget

Instagram offers two budget options: daily and lifetime. A daily budget allows you to set a daily limit for ad spend, while a lifetime budget allows you to set a total budget for the duration of your ad campaign. Choose a budget option that aligns with your business goals and ad objectives.

Bidding Strategies and Budget

Instagram offers two bidding strategies: cost per click (CPC) and cost per impression (CPM). CPC bidding allows you to pay for each click on your ad, while CPM bidding allows you to pay for every 1,000 impressions. Choose a bidding strategy that aligns with your ad objectives and budget.

Tips for Setting a Budget for Your Ad Campaigns

- Define your business goals and ad objectives
- Understand your target audience and their demographics, interests, and behaviors
- Research industry benchmarks to determine ad spend
- Choose a daily or lifetime budget option
- Select a bidding strategy that aligns with your ad objectives and budget
- Continuously monitor and optimize your ad campaigns to ensure maximum ROI

By setting a budget for your ad campaigns, you'll be able to reach your target audience, drive website traffic, generate sales, and build brand awareness. Remember to continuously monitor and optimize your ad campaigns to ensure maximum ROI.

CHAPTER 10

INFLUENCER MARKETING AND PARTNERSHIPS

UNDERSTANDING THE BENEFITS OF INFLUENCER MARKETING ON INSTAGRAM

In the realm of digital marketing, influencer marketing has emerged as a powerful tool for businesses to reach their target audience and build brand awareness. Instagram, with its vast user base and visual-centric platform, offers a fertile ground for influencer marketing to flourish. As an entrepreneur seeking to commercialize your Instagram presence, understanding the benefits of influencer marketing is crucial for your success.

Influencer marketing on Instagram allows you to partner with individuals who have built a loyal following on the platform. These influencers have established trust with their audience and can promote your products or services to their followers. By collaborating with influencers, you can tap into their network and reach a larger audience that may not have been possible through traditional advertising methods.

One of the primary benefits of influencer marketing on Instagram is its ability to increase brand awareness. When an influencer promotes your brand, their followers are exposed to your products or services, which can lead to a significant increase in brand recognition. This is especially true if the influencer has a highly engaged audience that trusts their recommendations.

In addition to increasing brand awareness, influencer marketing on Instagram can also drive website traffic and sales. By including a call-to-action in the influencer's post, such as "swipe up in the link in my bio," you can direct their followers to your website, where they can learn more about your products or services and make a purchase.

Influencer marketing on Instagram can also help you build credibility and trust with your target audience. When an influencer promotes your brand, it's like receiving a seal of approval from a trusted friend. This can be especially important for new businesses or those looking to establish themselves in a competitive industry.

Another significant benefit of influencer marketing on Instagram is its ability to provide social proof. When an influencer promotes your brand, it's like a virtual endorsement. Their followers see that someone they trust and respect is using and enjoying your products or services, which can increase the likelihood of them trying it out for themselves.

Influencer marketing on Instagram can also help you reach a niche audience that may be difficult to target through traditional advertising methods. Influencers often have a highly engaged audience that is interested in specific topics or industries, which can make them an ideal partner for businesses looking to target a specific demographic.

Furthermore, influencer marketing on Instagram can provide a high return on investment (ROI). According to a study by Tomoson, influencer marketing has an average ROI of $6.50 for every dollar spent. This is significantly higher than other forms of digital marketing, such as display advertising, which has an average ROI of $2.80 for every dollar spent.

In addition to the financial benefits, influencer marketing on Instagram can also provide a wealth of content for your business. Influencers often create high-quality content that can be repurposed for your brand's social media channels, website, and other marketing materials.

Finally, influencer marketing on Instagram can help you stay ahead of the competition. In today's digital landscape, businesses are constantly looking for new and innovative ways to reach their target audience. By partnering with influencers, you can stay ahead of the curve and establish your brand as a thought leader in your industry.

In conclusion, influencer marketing on Instagram offers a wealth of benefits for businesses looking to commercialize their presence on the platform. From increasing brand awareness and driving website traffic and sales, to building credibility and trust, providing social proof, and reaching a niche audience, influencer marketing can help you achieve your business goals. By partnering with influencers, you can tap into their network, reach a larger audience, and stay ahead of the competition. As an entrepreneur, understanding the benefits of influencer marketing on Instagram is crucial for your success, and learning how to take full advantage of it can be instrumental in moving you and your brand/business forward significantly in less time.

FINDING AND PARTNERING WITH INFLUENCERS IN YOUR NICHE

Finding and partnering with influencers in your niche is a crucial step in commercializing your Instagram presence. Influencer marketing allows you to reach a larger audience, build brand awareness, and drive sales. In this section, we'll delve into the details of finding and partnering with influencers in your niche, providing you with a comprehensive guide to help you commercialize your Instagram presence.

Identifying Influencers in Your Niche

Identifying influencers in your niche requires research and careful consideration. Start by defining your niche and what you're looking for in an influencer partnership. Consider factors such as reach, engagement, content quality, and audience demographics. Research influencers using tools such as Instagram's "Discover" page, influencer marketing platforms, and industry events.

Evaluating Influencer Suitability

Evaluating influencer suitability requires careful consideration of several factors, including their audience demographics, content quality, engagement rates, and brand alignment. Consider whether the influencer's audience aligns with your target market and whether their content resonates with your brand values. Evaluate their engagement rates to ensure they have an active and engaged audience.

Reach Out and Collaborate

Once you've identified and evaluated influencers in your niche, it's time to reach out and collaborate. Start by crafting a personalized message introducing your brand and proposing a collaboration. Be clear about what you're looking for in a partnership and what benefits the influencer can expect. Negotiate terms and ensure both parties are aligned on expectations.

Types of Influencer Collaborations

Influencer collaborations come in various forms, including sponsored posts, product reviews, giveaways, and ambassador programs. Sponsored posts involve paying influencers to promote your brand or product. Product reviews involve sending influencers free products in exchange for honest reviews. Giveaways involve partnering with influencers to give away products or services to their audience. Ambassador programs involve partnering with influencers for an extended period to promote your brand or product.

Tips for Finding and Partnering with Influencers

- Define your niche and what you're looking for in an influencer partnership
- Research influencers using various tools and platforms
- Evaluate influencer suitability based on audience demographics, content quality, engagement rates, and brand alignment
- Craft personalized messages when reaching out to influencers
- Negotiate terms and ensure both parties are aligned on expectations
- Consider various types of influencer collaborations
- Continuously monitor and optimize influencer partnerships to ensure maximum ROI

By finding and partnering with influencers in your niche, you'll be able to reach a larger audience, build brand awareness, and drive sales. Remember to continuously monitor and optimize influencer partnerships to ensure maximum ROI.

EXAMPLES OF INFLUENCERS YOU CAN COLLABORATE WITH IN DIFFERENT NICHES

Here are some examples of influencers in different niches based on their past collaborations:
Beauty and Cosmetics:

- NikkieTutorials (Nikkie de Jager) - Collaborated with brands like OFRA Cosmetics, Urban Decay, and Marc Jacobs Beauty

- James Charles - Collaborated with brands like Morphe, Urban Decay, and Kylie Cosmetics
- Tati Westbrook - Collaborated with brands like Halo Beauty, Drunk Elephant, and Anastasia Beverly Hills

Fashion:

- Chiara Ferragni - Collaborated with brands like Gucci, Chanel, and Louis Vuitton
- Olivia Palermo - Collaborated with brands like Valentino, Dior, and Stuart Weitzman
- Camila Coelho - Collaborated with brands like Dolce & Gabbana, Versace, and Balmain

Health and Wellness:

- Michelle Lewin - Collaborated with brands like Fit Tea, Bang Energy, and KetoLogic
- Jen Selter - Collaborated with brands like Nike, Adidas, and Fitbit
- Kayla Itsines - Collaborated with brands like Sweat, Fila, and Adidas

Travel:

- Mark Wiens - Collaborated with brands like Turkish Airlines, Marriott Hotels, and Visa
- The Blonde Abroad - Collaborated with brands like Hostelworld, Eurail, and Tourism Australia
- Expert Vagabond - Collaborated with brands like Patagonia, REI, and GoPro

Food and Beverage:

- David Chang - Collaborated with brands like Nike, Apple, and Coca-Cola

- Gordon Ramsay - Collaborated with brands like Hellmann's, Gordon Ramsay Home Cooking, and Royal Caribbean
- Ree Drummond - Collaborated with brands like Land O'Lakes, Kraft Foods, and Hyatt Hotels

Gaming:

- Ninja - Collaborated with brands like Red Bull, Ubisoft, and Samsung
- Dr. Disrespect - Collaborated with brands like G FUEL, ASUS, and Turtle Beach
- Shroud - Collaborated with brands like HyperX, Logitech G, and Alienware

Please note that these are just a few examples, and these are some of the most popular influencers in these niches, and so you may be unable to contact them for collaboration. However, there are many more influencers in each niche who have collaborated with various brands. So, keep searching and keep reaching out, and I assure you that you will find the perfect one suited to you based on you, your objectives and values and your budget.

BEST PRACTICES FOR INFLUENCER COLLABORATIONS AND SPONSORED CONTENT

When it comes to influencer collaborations and sponsored content on Instagram, there are several best practices that entrepreneurs should follow to ensure successful and effective partnerships. In this section, we'll delve into the details of these best practices, providing you with a comprehensive guide to help you commercialize your Instagram presence.

Authenticity and Relevance

Authenticity and relevance are crucial when it comes to influencer collaborations and sponsored content. Ensure that the influencers you partner with align with your brand values and target audience. Their content should resonate with your brand message, and their audience should be interested in your products or services. Authenticity is key to building trust with your audience, and relevance is essential for driving engagement and conversions.

Clear Communication

Clear communication is vital when collaborating with influencers. Ensure that you clearly outline the terms of the partnership, including the content requirements, posting schedule, and compensation. Be transparent about your brand's goals and expectations, and provide influencers with the necessary resources and support to create high-quality content.

High-Quality Content

High-quality content is essential for driving engagement and conversions on Instagram. Ensure that the content created by influencers is visually appealing, engaging, and aligns with your brand's aesthetic. Provide influencers with guidelines on the type of content you're looking for, and encourage them to use high-quality images and videos.

Disclosure and Transparency

Disclosure and transparency are crucial when it comes to sponsored content on Instagram. Ensure that influencers clearly disclose the partnership using hashtags like #ad, #sponsored, or #partner. This not only complies with Instagram's policies but also builds trust with your audience.

Long-Term Partnerships

Long-term partnerships with influencers can be highly effective for entrepreneurs. Instead of collaborating with influencers on a one-off basis, consider partnering with them for an extended period. This can help build a stronger relationship, increase brand awareness, and drive more conversions.

Influencer Takeovers

Influencer takeovers can be a great way to mix up your content and provide your audience with fresh perspectives. Consider partnering with influencers to take over your Instagram account for a day, where they can share their own content and engage with your audience.

Giveaways and Contests

Giveaways and contests can be highly effective for driving engagement and increasing brand awareness on Instagram. Consider partnering with influencers to host a giveaway or contest, where followers can enter to win a prize by following your account and tagging their friends.

Tracking and Measuring Performance

Tracking and measuring performance is crucial when it comes to influencer collaborations and sponsored content on Instagram. Use Instagram Insights to track engagement rates, reach, and conversions, and use this data to optimize your partnerships and content strategy.

By following these, entrepreneurs can ensure successful and effective influencer collaborations and sponsored content on Instagram. Remember to always prioritize authenticity and relevance, communicate clearly with influencers, and focus on creating high-quality content that resonates with your audience.

PART 4

Engagement and Community Building

CHAPTER 11
RESPONDING TO COMMENTS AND MESSAGES

UNDERSTANDING THE IMPORTANCE OF RESPONDING TO COMMENTS AND MESSAGES

Responding to comments and messages on Instagram is a crucial aspect of building a strong online presence and commercializing your account. As an entrepreneur, it's essential to understand the importance of engaging with your audience and responding to their queries, concerns, and feedback. In this section, we'll delve into the details of why responding to comments and messages is vital for your business and provide you with tips on how to do it effectively.

Building Trust and Credibility

Responding to comments and messages helps build trust and credibility with your audience. When you take the time to respond to their queries and concerns, you show them that you value their feedback and care about their needs. This helps establish a strong relationship with your audience, which can lead to increased loyalty, engagement, and ultimately, sales.

Improving Customer Service

Responding to comments and messages is an essential part of providing excellent customer service. By responding promptly to queries and concerns, you can resolve issues quickly and efficiently, which can lead to increased customer satisfaction and loyalty. This can also help reduce the risk of negative reviews and feedback, which can harm your business's reputation.

Encouraging Engagement

Responding to comments and messages can also encourage engagement on your account. When you respond to comments, you show your audience that you value their feedback and are willing to engage with them. This can lead to increased comments, likes, and shares, which can help increase your account's visibility and reach.

Providing Value

Responding to comments and messages provides value to your audience. By sharing your expertise, knowledge, and experience, you can help your audience solve problems, answer questions, and achieve their goals. This can help establish your business as a thought leader in your industry, which can lead to increased credibility and trust.

By responding to comments and messages, entrepreneurs can build trust and credibility with their audience, improve customer service, encourage engagement, and provide value. Remember to respond promptly, be authentic and transparent, and provide value in your responses.

TIPS FOR RESPONDING TO CUSTOMER INQUIRIES AND FEEDBACK

Responding to customer inquiries and feedback is a crucial aspect of building a strong online presence and commercializing your Instagram account. As an entrepreneur, it's essential to understand the importance of providing excellent customer service and responding to customer inquiries and feedback in a timely and effective manner. In this section, we'll delve into the details of tips for responding to customer inquiries and feedback, providing you with a comprehensive guide to help you commercialize your Instagram account.

Respond Promptly

Responding promptly to customer inquiries and feedback is essential. Customers expect a quick response, and delaying your response can lead to frustration and a negative experience. Aim to respond to customer inquiries and feedback within a few hours or at most, within 24 hours.

Be Personal and Authentic

When responding to customer inquiries and feedback, be personal and authentic. Address the customer by name, and use a conversational tone that reflects your brand's voice. Avoid using generic responses or automated messages that may come across as insincere.

Provide Clear and Concise Responses

Provide clear and concise responses that address the customer's inquiry or feedback. Avoid using jargon or technical terms that may confuse the customer. Instead, use simple language that is easy to understand.

Show Empathy and Apologize

Show empathy and apologize when necessary. If a customer has had a negative experience or has a complaint, acknowledge their feelings and apologize for any inconvenience caused. This shows that you value their feedback and are committed to providing excellent customer service.

Offer Solutions and Alternatives

Offer solutions and alternatives that meet the customer's needs. If a customer has a query or concern, provide a solution or alternative that addresses their issue. This shows that you are proactive and committed to providing excellent customer service.

Use Instagram's Built-in Features

Use Instagram's built-in features, such as polls and quizzes, to encourage engagement and gather feedback from customers. This can help you understand their needs and preferences, which can inform your customer service strategy.

Keep Records

Keep records of customer inquiries and feedback, including responses and resolutions. This can help you track patterns and trends, which can inform your customer service strategy and improve your overall performance.

Train Your Team

Train your team on how to respond to customer inquiries and feedback. Ensure that they understand the importance of providing excellent customer service and are equipped with the skills and knowledge to respond effectively.

Monitor and Measure Performance

Monitor and measure performance regularly, including response times, resolution rates, and customer satisfaction. This can help you identify areas for improvement and optimize your customer service strategy.

By following these tips, entrepreneurs can provide excellent customer service and respond to customer inquiries and feedback in a timely and effective manner. Remember to respond promptly, be personal and authentic, provide clear and concise responses, show empathy and apologize, offer solutions and alternatives, use Instagram's built-in features, keep records, train your team, and monitor and measure performance.

CHAPTER 12

HOSTING GIVEAWAYS AND CONTESTS

BENEFITS OF HOSTING GIVEAWAYS AND CONTESTS ON INSTAGRAM

Hosting giveaways and contests on Instagram can be a highly effective way for entrepreneurs to commercialize their account and achieve their business goals. By offering incentives and encouraging engagement, businesses can increase brand awareness, drive website traffic, generate leads, and build a loyal community of customers. In this section, we'll delve into the benefits of hosting giveaways and contests on Instagram, providing you with a comprehensive guide to help you commercialize your account.

Increased Brand Awareness

Hosting giveaways and contests on Instagram can help increase brand awareness by encouraging users to share your content, tag their friends, and use specific hashtags. This can lead to a significant increase in visibility, reaching a larger audience and potentially driving more sales.

Improved Engagement

Giveaways and contests can improve engagement on your account by encouraging users to like, comment, and share your content. This can lead to a significant increase in engagement rates, building a loyal community of customers who are interested in your products or services.

Driving Website Traffic

Hosting giveaways and contests on Instagram can drive website traffic by encouraging users to visit your website to enter the contest or redeem a prize. This can lead to a significant increase in website traffic, potentially driving more sales and conversions.

Generating Leads

Giveaways and contests can generate leads by encouraging users to provide their contact information to enter the contest or redeem a prize. This can lead to a significant increase in leads, potentially driving more sales and conversions.

Building a Loyal Community

Hosting giveaways and contests on Instagram can help build a loyal community of customers by encouraging users to engage with your content, share it with their friends, and tag their friends. This can lead to a significant increase in customer loyalty, potentially driving more sales and conversions.

Encouraging User-Generated Content

Giveaways and contests can encourage user-generated content by encouraging users to share their own content related to your brand. This can lead to a significant increase in user-generated content, potentially driving more engagement and brand awareness.

Increasing Reach

Hosting giveaways and contests on Instagram can increase reach by encouraging users to share your content, tag their friends, and use specific hashtags. This can lead to a significant increase in reach, potentially driving more brand awareness and sales.

Encouraging Collaboration

Giveaways and contests can encourage collaboration by partnering with other businesses or influencers to co-host a giveaway or contest. This can lead to a significant increase in collaboration, potentially driving more brand awareness and sales.

Building Trust and Credibility

Hosting giveaways and contests on Instagram can build trust and credibility by showing your audience that you're committed to providing value and rewarding their loyalty. This can lead to a significant increase in trust and credibility, potentially driving more sales and conversions.

Hosting giveaways and contests on Instagram can help you to increase brand awareness, improve engagement, drive website traffic, generate leads, build a loyal community, encourage user-generated content, increase reach, encourage collaboration, and build trust and credibility. Remember to always follow Instagram's guidelines and rules when hosting giveaways and contests, and to provide clear instructions and guidelines for participants in order to avoid any unnecessary complications in the future.

TIPS FOR HOSTING A SUCCESSFUL GIVEAWAY OR CONTEST

Hosting a successful giveaway or contest on Instagram can be a great way to commercialize your account, increase brand awareness, improve engagement, drive website traffic, generate leads, and build a loyal community of customers.

However, it's important to keep in mind that hosting a successful giveaway or contest requires careful planning and execution. In this section, we'll provide you with tips for hosting a successful giveaway or contest on Instagram, helping you to achieve your business goals.

Define Your Goals

Before hosting a giveaway or contest, it's important to define your goals. What do you want to achieve with your giveaway or contest? Do you want to increase brand awareness, improve engagement, drive website traffic, generate leads, or build a loyal community of customers? Knowing your goals will help you to create a giveaway or contest that is tailored to your needs.

Choose a Relevant Prize

The prize you choose for your giveaway or contest is crucial. It should be relevant to your business and appealing to your target audience. Choose a prize that is valuable and desirable, and that will encourage people to enter your giveaway or contest.

Set Clear Rules and Guidelines

It's important to set clear rules and guidelines for your giveaway or contest. This includes eligibility requirements, entry rules, and any other relevant details. Make sure your rules and guidelines are easy to understand and follow.

Use Relevant Hashtags

Hashtags are a great way to increase the visibility of your giveaway or contest. Use relevant hashtags that are related to your business and target audience. This will help your giveaway or contest to reach a larger audience and attract more entries.

Promote Your Giveaway or Contest

Promoting your giveaway or contest is crucial. Use your Instagram account to promote your giveaway or contest, and encourage your followers to share it with their friends and family. You can also use other social media channels, email marketing, and paid advertising to promote your giveaway or contest.

Partner with Other Businesses or Influencers

Partnering with other businesses or influencers can help to increase the reach and visibility of your giveaway or contest. Choose partners that are relevant to your business and target audience, and that have a large following on Instagram.

Use Instagram Stories and IGTV

Instagram Stories and IGTV are great ways to promote your giveaway or contest. Use these features to create engaging content that encourages people to enter your giveaway or contest.

Encourage User-Generated Content

Encouraging user-generated content is a great way to increase engagement and encourage people to enter your giveaway or contest. Ask people to share their own content related to your business or prize, and re-share it on your Instagram account.

Follow Instagram's Guidelines

It's important to follow Instagram's guidelines when hosting a giveaway or contest. Make sure you understand Instagram's rules and guidelines, and that you comply with them.

By following these tips, you can host a successful giveaway or contest on Instagram that helps you to achieve your business goals. Remember to define your goals, choose a relevant prize, set clear rules and guidelines, use relevant hashtags, promote your giveaway or contest, partner with other businesses or influencers, use Instagram Stories and IGTV, encourage user-generated content, and follow Instagram's guidelines.

PART 5

Analytics and Tracking

CHAPTER 13

UNDERSTANDING INSTAGRAM INSIGHTS

UNDERSTANDING INSTAGRAM INSIGHTS AND THEIR BENEFITS

Understanding Instagram Insights and their benefits is crucial for businesses, influencers, and individuals who want to optimize their Instagram presence and drive more engagement and growth on the platform. Instagram Insights is a free analytics tool that provides valuable data about the performance of your account, including engagement rates, reach, impressions, and audience demographics. By analyzing this data, you can make informed decisions about your content strategy, identify trends in your audience behavior, and drive more successful outcomes overall on the platform.

Instagram Insights provides detailed information about your audience, including age, gender, location, and interests. You can also view data about your audience's behavior, like when they're most active on the platform and what types of content they engage with the most. By understanding your audience and their behavior, you can optimize your content strategy to reach them at the right time and with the right content.

In addition, Instagram Insights provides valuable information about how many people have interacted with your content. This metric is known as reach, and it measures the total number of unique accounts that have seen your posts or stories. You can also view data about different types of reach, including organic reach and paid reach. By analyzing your reach data, you can identify which types of posts, stories, or reels are resonating with your audience and which ones are not.

Instagram Insights also supplies detailed information about how your audience is engaging with your content, including likes, shares, saves, comments, and more. You can also view your engagement rate, which is the percentage of people who engage with your content compared to the total number of people who see it. By tracking your engagement over time, you can identify trends and patterns in your audience's behavior and adjust your content strategy accordingly.

Moreover, Instagram Insights has information on the number of likes, comments, shares, saves, and views for each individual post. This data can be used to determine which posts are performing well and which ones are not. By analyzing this data, you can adjust your content strategy to create more effective content and drive more engagement.

Instagram Insights also provides data about your website clicks, which is critical if you're trying to drive traffic and sales to your website. You can view the number of people who are clicking on the link in your bio and visiting your website. By tracking website clicks on Instagram, you can evaluate the effectiveness of your call-to-action and adjust your content strategy to better drive traffic and sales.

If you're running paid advertising campaigns on Instagram, you can also view data about ad performance, such as the number of clicks, conversions, and revenue generated by the ad. Through this data, you can evaluate the effectiveness of your paid advertising campaigns and optimize them for better results.

By using Instagram Insights, you can identify successful posts and campaigns, optimize your publishing schedule, improve your understanding of your target audience's preferences, and determine how to expand or refine your niche. You can also use Instagram Insights to track your account growth, engagement rates, and audience demographics over time, allowing you to make data-driven decisions and drive more successful outcomes on the platform.

Instagram Insights is a powerful tool that provides valuable data about your account performance, audience behavior, and content performance. By analyzing this data, you can optimize your content strategy, identify trends in your audience behavior, and drive more successful outcomes on the platform. Whether you're a business, influencer, or individual, understanding Instagram Insights and their benefits is crucial for achieving success

NAVIGATING THE INSTAGRAM INSIGHTS DASHBOARD

Navigating the Instagram Insights dashboard can seem overwhelming at first, but once you understand the different sections and metrics, you'll be able to use the data to optimize your content strategy and drive more successful outcomes on the platform. In this section, we'll break down the different sections of the Instagram Insights dashboard and provide tips on how to use the data to improve your Instagram presence.

Account Overview

The Account Overview section provides a snapshot of your account's performance over the past seven days. You'll see metrics such as account reach, impressions, and engagement. This section also shows your average engagement rate and average watch time for videos.

Content Section

The Content section shows data about individual posts, stories, and reels. You can view metrics such as engagement, reach, and impressions for each piece of content. This section also shows which types of content are performing well and which ones need improvement.

Audience Section

The Audience section provides data about your followers, including age, gender, location, and interests. You can also view metrics such as follower growth and audience demographics.

Engagement Section

The Engagement section shows data about how your audience is interacting with your content. You can view metrics such as likes, comments, saves, and shares. This section also shows which types of content are driving the most engagement.

Reach Section

The Reach section shows data about how many people are seeing your content. You can view metrics such as account reach, impressions, and reach rate.

Videos Section

The Videos section shows data about your video content, including views, watch time, and engagement.

Shopping Section

The Shopping section shows data about your shopping posts and stories, including views, clicks, and purchases.

IGTV Section

The IGTV section shows data about your IGTV content, including views, watch time, and engagement.

Stories Section

The Stories section shows data about your stories, including views, swipes, and replies.

Reels Section

The Reels section shows data about your reels, including views, watch time, and engagement.

By navigating the Instagram Insights dashboard and understanding the different sections and metrics, you'll be able to use the data to optimize your content strategy and drive more successful outcomes on the platform. Remember to track your metrics over time, identify trends and patterns in your data, and adjust your content strategy accordingly. With Instagram Insights, you'll be able to make data-driven decisions and drive more engagement, reach, and sales on Instagram.

UNDERSTANDING METRICS AND DIMENSIONS

Understanding metrics and dimensions is crucial for businesses and entrepreneurs who want to commercialize their Instagram presence and drive more successful outcomes on the platform. Instagram provides a range of metrics and dimensions that help you understand how your content is performing, how your audience is engaging with your brand, and how to optimize your content strategy for better results.

Reach and Impressions

Reach and impressions are two of the most important metrics on Instagram. Reach refers to the number of unique accounts that have seen your posts or stories, while impressions refer to the total number of times your content has been viewed. Understanding reach and impressions helps you understand how many people are seeing your content and how often they're seeing it.

Engagement

Engagement refers to the number of likes, comments, saves, shares, and reactions on your posts and stories. Engagement metrics help you understand how your audience is interacting with your content and how to optimize your content strategy for better engagement.

Dimensions

Dimensions refer to the specific characteristics of your audience, such as age, gender, location, interests, and behaviors. Understanding dimensions helps you understand who your audience is, what they're interested in, and how to create content that resonates with them.

Average Watch Time

Average watch time refers to the amount of time people spend watching your videos. This metric helps you understand how engaging your video content is and how to optimize it for better results.

Follower Growth Rate

Follower growth rate refers to the rate at which your follower count is increasing or decreasing. This metric helps you understand how your content strategy is impacting your follower growth and how to adjust it for better results.

Account Reach Rate

Account reach rate refers to the percentage of your followers who are seeing your content. This metric helps you understand how many of your followers are actively engaging with your brand and how to optimize your content strategy for better reach.

Average Engagement Rate

Average engagement rate refers to the percentage of people who engage with your content after seeing it. This metric helps you understand how engaging your content is and how to optimize it for better results.

By understanding metrics and dimensions on Instagram, you can optimize your content strategy, increase engagement, reach, and sales, and drive more successful outcomes on the platform. Remember to track your metrics over time, identify trends and patterns in your data, and adjust your content strategy accordingly.

USING INSTAGRAM INSIGHTS TO TRACK WEBSITE TRAFFIC AND CONVERSIONS

Using Instagram Insights to track website traffic and conversions is a vital component of any business's Instagram marketing strategy. Instagram Insights, also known as Instagram Analytics, provides businesses with valuable data and information about their audience, engagement rates, and website traffic. With this information, businesses can refine their marketing strategy, increase engagement, and drive more website traffic and conversions.

The first step in using Instagram Insights to track website traffic and conversions is to switch to a business profile. This can be done by accessing the settings page on the Instagram app, tapping "Account," and selecting "Switch to Professional Account." From there, users can choose their category and connect their Facebook page if desired.

Once a business profile is set up, users can access Instagram Insights, which provides an overview of account performance, including accounts reached, accounts engaged, total followers, and content shared. The "Accounts Reached" section provides more specific information about the users who have seen a business's content and interacted with their profile, including reached audience, follower status, gender, age, countries, and cities.

In addition to the Insights Overview, Instagram Insights also provides information about individual posts and stories, including engagement rates, reach, and clicks on links and call-to-action buttons. This information can be used to identify which types of content are most effective at driving website traffic and conversions and to refine a business's content strategy accordingly.

To track website traffic and conversions using Instagram Insights, businesses can use the "Swipe-Up" feature in Instagram Stories, which allows users to add a link to their story that followers can click on to visit their website. Businesses can also add links to their bio and use Instagram's shopping feature to tag products directly in their posts and stories.

In addition to Instagram Insights, businesses can also use third-party analytics tools, such as Google Analytics, to track website traffic and conversions. Google Analytics provides more detailed information about website traffic, including the number of visitors, page views, bounce rate, and conversion rate. By using both Instagram Insights and Google Analytics, businesses can get a more complete picture of their website traffic and conversions and make data-driven decisions to optimize their marketing strategy.

UTM tagging is another effective method for tracking website traffic and conversions. UTM tagging involves adding a piece of code to the end of a URL that enables businesses to track certain parameters in their Google Analytics dashboard, such as traffic source. By using UTM tagging, businesses can identify which campaigns and content are driving the most website traffic and conversions and optimize their marketing strategy accordingly.

In conclusion, using Instagram Insights to track website traffic and conversions is a crucial component of any business's Instagram marketing strategy. By providing valuable data and information about audience engagement, content performance, and website traffic, Instagram Insights enables businesses to refine their marketing strategy, increase engagement, and drive more website traffic and conversions. By combining Instagram Insights with third-party analytics tools, such as Google Analytics, and UTM tagging, businesses can get a more complete picture of their website traffic and conversions and make data-driven decisions to optimize their marketing strategy.

CONCLUSION

Congratulations on getting to the end of this simple guide. In "How to Use Instagram for Business in 2024: The Entrepreneur's Definitive Guide for Commercializing Instagram Today," we have covered the essential strategies and techniques for leveraging Instagram to grow your business. From setting up an optimized profile to creating engaging content and utilizing Instagram Stories and Reels, we have explored the various features and tools that Instagram offers for businesses.

Key takeaways from the guide include:

- Creating an Instagram Business profile unlocks exclusive features such as Instagram Insights, contact information, and action buttons.
- Developing a solid Instagram marketing strategy involves defining your target audience, setting goals and KPIs, tracking performance, and creating a content calendar.
- Posting high-quality content, utilizing hashtags, and engaging with your audience are crucial for increasing brand awareness and driving website traffic and sales.
- Instagram Stories and Reels offer unique opportunities for businesses to share behind-the-scenes content, sneak peeks, and exclusive deals.
- Collaborating with influencers, running Instagram Ads, and utilizing Instagram's shopping feature can expand your reach and drive conversions.

As Instagram continues to evolve, businesses can expect new features and tools to emerge, providing even more opportunities for growth and engagement. Some potential future developments on the horizon include:

- Enhanced e-commerce capabilities, such as augmented reality shopping and more seamless checkout experiences.
- Increased focus on community building, with features like Instagram's "Close Friends" feature and enhanced group chat capabilities.
- Greater emphasis on video content, with the continued rise of Instagram Reels and potentially even more video-centric features.
- Further integration with other Meta platforms, such as Facebook and WhatsApp, to provide a more comprehensive marketing and engagement experience.
- Businesses that stay ahead of the curve and adapt to these changes will be well-positioned to thrive on Instagram and reach their target audiences in innovative and effective ways.

Additional Resources for Further Learning:

For entrepreneurs seeking to further enhance their Instagram skills and stay up-to-date on the latest best practices, the following resources are recommended:

- Instagram for Business: A comprehensive guide provided by Instagram itself, covering topics like setting up a business profile, creating content, and running ads.
- Hootsuite Academy: A free online resource offering courses and certifications on social media marketing, including Instagram-specific training.
- Social Media Examiner: A leading industry publication providing news, tips, and strategies for social media marketing professionals.
- Influencer Marketing Hub: A platform offering insights, tools, and resources for businesses partnering

with influencers on Instagram and other social media channels.
- Sprout Social: A social media management and analytics tool providing businesses with data-driven insights to optimize their Instagram marketing efforts.

By leveraging these resources and staying informed about the latest developments on Instagram, entrepreneurs can ensure they are maximizing their potential on this powerful social media platform.

www.ingramcontent.com/pod-product-compliance
Lightning Source LLC
Chambersburg PA
CBHW031548080326
40690CB00054B/745